Frank Meadows has a passion for b
wise, full of God, and has been a n
most 40 years. In this powerful book, *Jesus, Healer of the Brokenhearted*, he shares the "God-designed pathways and principles" for each of us to understand and respond to fear, anxiety, shame, anger, and any other emotional struggles we face to get the breakthroughs we desire. Read this book and allow God to minister freedom, peace and joy to your heart!

HEIDI G. BAKER, PHD

Co-Founder and CEO of Iris Global
Bestselling author of *Birthing the Miraculous*

Is there any one of us who has not experienced either loss, trauma, abuse or adversity at some point in our lives? I don't think so. We grit our teeth, stuff our feelings, and think we have survived. Life is about more than just surviving. Jesus said the whole reason He came was for us "to have life, and have it abundantly!" If you are not living an abundant life, full of God's blessings and joy, and free of the past, then this book is for you! I have known Frank Meadows and the work he does for years, and have seen the truths and the healing he writes about touch and change lives within my own family. Don't settle for simply surviving when God offers you abundance. Read this book with expectancy and anticipation, and embark on your own journey to wholeness and freedom. Thank you, Frank Meadows, for making it so attainable!

TERRY MEEUWSEN

Co-host, The 700 Club
Founder, Orphan's Promise
Author of *The God Adventure: Embracing His Power and Purpose for You* and
Near to the Heart of God: God's Words of Encouragement for Women

I strongly believe that powerful revelations in this book will change and transform many lives. This is a much needed work that impacted my life personally in a great way. I'm very glad to see it's made available to everyone who is seeking inner healing and freedom. I believe it's also going to be a great tool for those who want to be used to help others in their journey to find freedom.

ISIK ABLA

Founder, Isik Abla Ministries
Host of "Embracing New Life"
Winner of the 2017 National Religious Broadcasters International Impact Award
Author of *I Dreamed Freedom*

Frank Meadows has served as an Elder since 2011 at Big House Church, a congregation in Norfolk, Virginia, where I pastor. I have never met someone so devoted to the process of spiritual and emotional healing as Frank. My wife and I have both received ministry from Frank that has been nothing short of revolutionary in both of our lives. Frank invites us to welcome Holy Spirit into every corner of our hearts, especially those broken and wounded places. Rather than run from our personal pain, we journey to the center of it, hand in hand with Jesus, where He reveals His truth to our anguish, anger and apathy. The freedom accessible to each of us in Christ is nothing short of miraculous. Frank's methods and ministry empower the Jesus-follower to abandon a victim mentality in exchange for a victorious one. In his new book, Frank takes us on an exciting journey that leads us through our brokenness into newfound joy and peace in Christ Jesus that we may have thought was never possible.

ADAM CATES

Pastor, Big House Church
Norfolk, Virginia

This book is teaming with life and hope for those stuck in cycles of defeat and brokenness. It's a must-read for both those who desire to walk in a greater place of freedom and wholeness as well as those who feel called to be more effective ministers of healing. This book isn't just a collection of nice theories but is full of practical wisdom and revelation that Frank has mined through over forty years of healing ministry. The content is rich, and weighty but conveyed in a practical and relational format. I believe you will feel empowered and equipped at a whole new level after reading this incredible resource!

DAVID FRITCH

Director, Burn 24-7 Field Training

Author of *"Enthroned"*

As a pastor, I cannot emphasize enough the importance of this book for the Body of Christ. We all have things that happen in our lives that shape the way we lead, react and interact with each other. It is important as disciples that we believe and pursue the complete life (*sozo*) that Jesus offers us. Frank, with years of experience and revelation in the area of inner healing, gives us keys that will help everyone come to know the birthright of freedom given to each of us. My prayer for this book is the very same prayer we find that John prayed. In this book, Frank unlocks this scripture and how we can have a healthy soul through Christ...

> *"Beloved, I pray that you may prosper in all things and be in health, just as your soul prospers."*

3 JOHN 1:2, NKJV

Frank has helped me, my family, our staff and church walk in the health that Christ promised. It is my great joy to recommend this book to you. May it bring hope and freedom to places in your life that once held you back.

AARON KENNEDY

Lead Pastor, Opendoor Church

Winterville, North Carolina

Jesus, Healer of the Brokenhearted, is a remarkable, life-changing guide for every believer to experience deeper freedom, wholeness, and peace in Jesus. Provides you a practical process to overcoming deep, debilitating, lie-based beliefs through Mind Renewing Healing Prayer. Discover how emotional pain triggers are invaluable clues to help you replace lie-based thinking with the deep healing and wholeness only found in Jesus Christ's truth. This is a uniquely biblical, practical, and powerful spiritual guide with proven results.

DAN CHAVERIN

Executive Pastor and Church Consultant, Westside Family Church
Lenexa, Kansas

JESUS

HEALER OF THE
BROKENHEARTED

Discovering the Pathway to Healing
Through Spirit-led Mind Renewal

Frank Meadows

Cover Design by RedDove Design
Interior Design by Scottie A.B.

ISBN: 978-1-947165-62-5

Printed in the United States.

JESUS

HEALER OF THE

BROKENHEARTED

Discovering the Pathway to Healing
Through Spirit-led Mind Renewal

Frank Meadows

TABLE OF CONTENTS

FOREWORD

BY TONY STOLTZFUS

One of the great breakthroughs of my life came in a healing session with Frank. I had loaned my life savings to a good friend in ministry, and it took years to get the money back. In addition to destroying our relationship and shared ministry, I ended up having to leave my life's work to that point and start over. As Frank and I processed through the pain, I kept coming back to the question "Why?" Why had I not seen it sooner? Why had I stayed in such an abusive situation? Why had I enabled and avoided and agreed instead of challenging and confronting?

Then I found the answer. I had a deeply held, unspoken belief: "If the relationship is broken, something is wrong with me." And then another one: I believed that reaching my destiny was dependent on the favor of this leader. I had made excuses, enabled and avoided because I was afraid of losing my integrity and my future.

I renounced my old beliefs, invited Jesus to meet me there, and then I changed—profoundly. I don't believe I would be capable of doing what I do today in ministry without that encounter. I coach "senior leaders in painful transitions"—often high-powered people in the most difficult moments of their lives. Sometimes what they need from me is a difficult, honest, direct conversation about what they need to change. I couldn't do that before. I was too afraid of losing my integrity by losing the relationship to give that kind of challenge. But now that I'm free, I can do it powerfully, confidently, and without the personal baggage that would make it easy to be written off.

I am a huge believer in inner healing. My wife and I have benefitted from it for over 30 years, and I've done it off and on with Frank for the last 15 because he is the best practitioner I've ever found. I've referred a lot of leaders to him, and they've been deeply impacted as well. So I am very happy that he has finally put down on paper his methods and philosophy—and some of his stories!—to share with you.

A big reason I love healing prayer is that it pretty consistently produces pretty dramatic results. Although I can get lost in my head sometimes (hey, I'm a guy!), I always leave our sessions changed. In fact, the encounters at the heart of this method are the easiest, most effective way to produce transformation I know of. I've gotten to where I love it when my problems turn out to be inner healing issues, because I know I can go to Jesus and get immediate relief and dramatic change for very little effort.

I've probably coached 1,000 ministry leaders over the last 20 years, and one of the great sorrows of my life as a coach is working with leaders who seem closed to even the possibility of emotional healing. We'll discover that their past pain is influencing their present behavior (the #1 clue that you need healing), but when I ask, "What do you want to do about that?" I get vague, resigned excuses. "There's nobody nearby I can talk to" is a favorite line pastors use to opt out of getting whole—in reality, they are afraid of what might happen if it gets out that they struggle with hurt or betrayal. Or, "I saw a counselor once, but it didn't really help." Or, surprisingly often, "I'll find some scriptures about this and declare (or recite, or memorize) them."

The problem with that approach is that engaging the *logos* (the rational word) touches your rational brain, but your healing issues reside in your emotional brain. Rational-brain tools like reciting scripture are good for renewing the rational mind but aren't very effective at dealing with emotional wounds. Your emotional brain speaks the language of image and experience, so it takes an experiential word—a *rhema*, a personal encounter with God—to change it.

That's why healing prayer is so different from the traditional counseling I've been through. Instead of analyzing the problem rationally and prescribing action steps to change it, healing prayer facilitates an experiential encounter with Jesus that directly touches the emotional brain. Our biggest giants and the things we most struggle to overcome as Christians don't originate in the rational but in the emotional sphere. When we employ emotional-brain tools to face those giants, we get the kind of results the New Testament promises.

This one insight—that it takes an experiential encounter to touch the emotional brain—has totally changed the way I coach. Instead of analyzing the problem with my coachees, I've learned to help them have a desire-filling conversation with Jesus instead. That living encounter touches them in ways I never could.

The supernatural is essential to Christianity. And it is far easier to access than we've made it out to be. Healing prayer is a great way to give your heart a supernatural touch and to see the supernatural results it brings.

– TONY STOLTZFUS

Executive Director of Leadership MetaFormation

He has been a Master Coach for nearly 20 years and has founded multiple coach training schools.

He is the author of 10 books, including the best-selling *Coaching Questions.*

ACKNOWLEDGMENTS

Countless days of writing and thousands of cups of coffee pour overs from the great baristas from Café Moka and Cure Coffeehouse have transpired since I began this project. First and foremost, I would like to give all the praise and glory to Jesus for inspiring, equipping, motivating and giving me the discipline and anointing through the Holy Spirit to write this book!

I am so blessed and thankful for my wonderful wife, Beth, for giving me the grace, prayers, encouragement, as well as the freedom and time to write. She is my best friend and has been my greatest supporter throughout my adult life; I can't imagine doing life without her! Many thanks to my great sons, Jon and Ryan, and my wonderful daughter-in-law, Catherine. Thanks for your support and encouragement! I'm so thankful that I had a godly, loving dad, Wayne, who is now with Jesus and a great mom, Maryalice Meadows. She has always been a great, lifelong prayer warrior for me and my family, even now at 85. A special thanks to her as she has been diligent in prayer and encouragement!

I also want to give a special shout out of thanks and appreciation to my cousin George Moser, whom I have always admired, and his late wife, Joanne. Thanks for always being there for me as a wayward teen who went off the deep end. Thank you for praying for me and for being present the night I accepted Christ at the coffee house in Youngstown at 19. Thank you for starting the Bible study soon after, where many teens met Christ and where I met and fell in love with my wife, Beth. Most of all, thank you for unbelievably donating a kidney to my dad for his transplant. *"No one has greater love [no one has shown stronger affection] than to lay down (give up) his own life for his friends"* (JOHN 15:13, AMPC). Your life has personified this verse! An eternal thank-you! Any treasure I lay up in heaven is also credited to your account!

Also, an appreciative shout out to all the intercessory prayer warriors, too many to name, who have prayed for me throughout this project, especially from Big House Church. Special thanks to Dorothy Jones, Leslie Chaverin, Jerry Cates and Deb Porter for your continued prayer support and diligent intercession! I'm eternally grateful! Many thanks to my pastors, Adam and Lindsey Cates, for your prayers and encouragement and for supporting me, my ministry and this writing project. Thanks, Adam, for your friendship and for cultivating such a creative atmosphere of Presence-based worship at Big House Church, which has surely helped me find my creative niche!

Thanks to Susan Thompson of Revelation Publishing House for guiding and consulting with me and for connecting me to my great editor, Amanda Vigneaud. Thanks, Amanda, not only for your great editing skills, but for you interest in this project, insight and wisdom beyond your years. I can't thank you enough!

Many thanks to Lexi Banales from Printopya, who guided me through the quagmire of the publishing process.

Also, thanks to Nick Wallace from Red Dove Designs for the great cover graphics.

Many thanks to Dr. Ed Smith for mentoring, teaching and grounding me long ago in the Theophostic Healing Prayer principles. It equipped me, changed my ministry, and helped establish a foundation for the tools I operate in today.

Finally, many thanks to the thousands of people I've had the great privilege of ministering Mind Renewing Healing Prayer to over the years. You have taught me as well and allowed me to learn and grow from our work together. I've learned so much from you, co-laboring with the Lord as the Holy Spirit helped me fashion my healing gifts.

INTRODUCTION

NOTE FROM THE AUTHOR

Are you discouraged and seeking a breakthrough in your life? Maybe you have tried therapy, self-help books or other treatment, but you are still hurting. If you are in need of a healing, why not consider the wholeness that only Jesus can offer? This book is primarily for people in need of personal healing and transformation and who are open to a Christian world view. The principles in this book are predicated totally and completely upon a Christian world view, the Bible, God's written Word, which is His revelation to humankind, His beloved children. Jesus is alive and active in our lives today, and this concept is central to this book. Jesus is the *living Word* that became flesh and dwelt among us. God is not dead, but He is alive, contrary to what some may say. I experience Him daily when I minister to countless people and co-labor with Him. He uses me as a vessel as He brings miraculous healing truth to the wounded, hurt and broken. Many Christians in need of a healing breakthrough have not fully understood the simple but powerful salvation made available for us through Jesus. We have been blessed with the gift of the Holy Spirit, through which He ministers, heals and strengthens us.

Jesus, the God-man, came into this world so that God could reveal Himself and His love to us. Many do not understand that we are created for intimacy with God. Without spiritual intimacy with our Creator, we walk through life with a hole in our soul. Something is missing, and we often don't know what we lack or why. We fill the hole with the wrong things, seeking to fill our emptiness and spiritual void. We medicate with Mood-altering compulsive behaviors, relationships, success and material things. Ultimately, trying to satisfy our brokenness in these ways is like filling our car with water instead of fuel and expecting it to run properly; the holes in our souls cannot be filled with anything apart from God.

As Christians, we need to read carefully the Bible, our Heavenly Designer's manual. In it, God showed us His love so that we could be redeemed from the sinful state that separated us from Him. He died so we could be connected to Him, now and forevermore! As a part of our covenant of salvation, God planned to heal, renew and restore His creation. This unbelievable plan included provision to redeem, renew and restore us by healing us and putting us in right relationship with Him. Through the cross, *God provided for our healing, mind renewal and restoration.*

> *"And may the God of peace Himself sanctify you through and through [separate you from profane things, make you pure and wholly consecrated to God]; and may your spirit and soul and body be preserved sound and complete [and found] blameless at the coming of our Lord Jesus Christ (the Messiah)."*
>
> (1 THESSALONIANS 5:23, AMP)

We are all wounded and broken, some almost beyond repair. Humanity is far more in need of a savior than we will ever know. The good news is that the healing, mind renewing power of Jesus Christ is available for *all who will receive Him.* If we receive Jesus as our Savior and Lord, we open the door to all the covenant promises of God in our lives.

> *"But as many as received Him, to them He gave the right to become children of God, to those who believe in His name."*
>
> (JOHN 1:12, NKJV)

The purpose of this book is to understand the problem of the human condition in our broken state and to teach readers how to receive its remedy practically. I believe the solution to the broken state of humanity is the life-saving power of the triune God, who provides all we need to walk in healing, mind renewal, restoration and wholeness. When we know Him and receive all He has to offer, we become whole, fully able to fulfill our destiny, life purpose and calling.

PART ONE

THE FOUNDATIONS OF MIND RENEWING HEALING PRAYER

CHAPTER 1

FROM VICTIM TO VICTOR, FROM WOUNDED TO WARRIOR

"In the beginning was the Word, and the Word was with God, and the Word was God...And the Word became flesh and dwelt among us, and we beheld His glory, the glory as of the only begotten of the Father, full of grace and truth."
(JOHN 1:1,14, NKJV)

HEALING PRINCIPLE: We are all wounded and broken, some almost beyond repair. However, God has made provision for our healing, mind renewal, and restoration through Jesus Christ. Healing is available to all who will receive Jesus Christ as Lord and Savior.

For many years, I have worked as a mental health professional, licensed clinical social worker, and psychotherapist in a Christian counseling setting. I have helped thousands of people wrestle through many psychological, mental and relational problems. Many have come for help, experiencing difficulties with their marriages, parenting, depression, anxiety, bipolar disorders, and a myriad of various psychological problems. I have counseled and ministered to many who have been victims of sexual, physical, emotional, psychological and spiritual trauma and abuse.

My desire has always been to integrate sound biblical principles, under the guidance and direction of the Holy Spirit, with sound psychological concepts to help move people from victimhood into victory. In order to maximize the healing of the brokenhearted, I believe the therapist or healing prayer minister must operate in the gifts and power of the Holy Spirit. God intends for those who minister healing to bring nothing less than the full measure of the gospel of Jesus Christ to those to whom we minister. He fully expects and intends for us to receive the message of the power of the cross and the shed blood of Jesus to manifest in our own lives so it can witness to those receiving ministry. For this reason, the therapist must flow in the gifts and power of the Holy Spirit.

My journey in healing began when I was quite young. In retrospect, I can see God's call on my life from an early age. I was raised in an evangelical, Free Methodist Christian tradition where my father was a pastor for many years. As I look back on my life, I can see the Lord's fingerprints on my destiny, even though I was unaware of it as a youth. When in college, my studies gave me the opportunity to move deeper into the calling God had placed on my life. I attended Spring Arbor College (now Spring Arbor University), a Christian liberal arts school in Spring Arbor, Michigan. I was raised in an evangelical, biblical tradition that was not oriented to a charismatic experience. Somehow, even though this was not in my particular stream of Christianity, I found myself drawn to books on inner healing early in my college years, such as *Healing for Damaged Emotions* by David A. Seamands, and other related books. I now understand that was God wooing me toward

Spirit-led, inner healing prayer.

In 1999, a major shift occurred in my counseling ministry. I came across a healing approach called Theophostic Healing Prayer (TPM) that changed everything for me. After training with the TPM founder, Dr. Ed Smith, I discovered we had lived in the same college dorm in 1973 at Spring Arbor University. We were shocked to discover that we knew many of the same people from our time at university, but, now in our mid-forties, we did not recognize one another. Not long after we reconnected, I invited him to my house where we dug out the 1973-74 Spring Arbor yearbook from my attic. He immediately recognized me in the photos as the slender kid with shoulder-length, light-brown hair, and I recognized him as well. That marked the beginning of a great relationship. I had the privilege of traveling to Ghana with Dr. Smith in 2006 for his first live ministry training trip in Africa. It was an honor to spend that trip ministering to broken leaders, pastors and counselors there. Ever since I discovered these powerful healing prayer principles, my life has not been the same.

From the time I began using healing prayer principles, I have been honored to work with the Lord and to witness Him heal many wounded people, including pastors, missionaries and church leaders. Since 1999, I have prayed with individuals through thousands of traumatic memories where lie-based core beliefs have taken root in the prayer recipient's childhood. Co-laboring with Jesus, time and time again, I have had the privilege of working with the Lord as He has displaced thousands of lie-based beliefs, rooted in the prayer recipient's wounded memories, with His truth. I have witnessed many people experience complete healing of the memories we visit. What an honor it has been for me to work alongside Jesus and the Holy Spirit! How awesome it is to be able to minister to so many wounded, broken people on their healing journey and to see them released into their true identity and destiny.

Throughout my journey in this field, I have watched countless people leave victimhood behind to walk in the victory the Lord has made available through His death, shed blood and resurrection. No longer wounded, and understanding the depths of what it means to overcome difficulty, they receive their healing and assume their roles as mighty warriors in His kingdom. This is both the goal and the end result of the Lord's inner healing. It is awesome to behold.

Since I began my work in this field, more and more people have received healing and restoration through Mind Renewing Healing Prayer. The word has spread, and people have started to come from around the country; some have even traveled internationally to receive prayer from my ministry. I have had the privilege of teaching and ministering Mind Renewing Healing Prayer in Turkey and three different African countries, including in Mozambique through Heidi and Roland Baker's Iris Ministries. This healing process works here at home and even in the far reaches of the globe through interpreters! I have learned that Jesus always shows up to heal the brokenhearted, whom He loves with all His heart, because God's love is vaster than we will ever comprehend. He desires, and has made provision, that we might let His massive heart absorb our hurt as He releases His healing balm through His truth.

Many years after having studied with Dr. Smith and his wife, Sharon, I still highly recommend the Theophostic Healing Prayer training now called TPM. His work has deeply influenced my thinking and I have integrated it into my work and ministry. I have incorporated minor variations into this approach and have found it very helpful over the years as I have launched my own ministry. It is my heart to share my experiences in healing with the body of Christ, as well as to those who are open to Christ. Much of the TPM principles, and specifically the key concept of lie-based beliefs, are the root of many present-day problems. Healing and renewing our mind's foundational, lie-based beliefs are always at the core of this healing process.

Before delving into the details of the healing process, it is important to note that while my healing ministry is rooted in Theophostic principles, my approach slightly differs from TPM. While I make reference to Theophostic concepts throughout the book, I will refer to the healing process I use as Mind Renewing Healing Prayer. Some of the ways my healing process differs from TPM is in my approach to deal with vows, curses, and judgments, which I believe open us to demonization and need to be dealt with to accelerate one's healing. I will explain these differences more when I detail the Mind Renewing Healing Prayer process later in this book.

Jesus, Healer of the Brokenhearted is the foundational work in a forthcoming series. I have written extensively over the past 4 years, and I have much more to share in future volumes.

This book details Mind Renewing Healing Prayer and how the process works in ministry. In it, you will find helpful tips to deal with issues and questions that consistently occur during healing sessions, such as emotional triggers, lie-based thinking, free will, defense mechanisms, and demonization. Despite the theme of this book, please bear in mind that my ministry focus is not only the Mind Renewing Healing Prayer process, but the many Spirit-led tributaries that flow into the river of healing.[1]

This book will be helpful to the healing prayer minister and mental health professional, *but it is primarily written for the person searching for the pathway to their own healing journey, to those desiring genuine freedom, release and breakthrough!*

I believe the concepts in this book can change your life, propel you forward, and release you into your God-given destiny as you apply these healing principles to your life. We all develop our own unique ways of ministering to others as we co-labor with God. Mind Renewing Healing Prayer is one of the unique ways I minister with Him. The Lord desires for us to join Him as co-workers, using our unique personalities and gifts, so I invite you to use the resources in this book to learn to minister with and receive from Him in this way if you so desire.

---

[1] When I teach, I find it very important to explain that I do not make suggestions during prayer sessions with regards to guiding memory content, nor do I give prophetic words or words of knowledge during a Mind Renewing Healing Prayer session. I believe the gifts of the Holy Spirit operate during healing sessions, but it is not my role to suggest memory content to the person who has experienced brokenness and trauma. Instead, following a healing session, I may pray prophetically over the prayer recipient after they have resolved their memories with God. Even then, I am careful not to suggest memory content or discuss what I think may have happened to them in their past. Many report this is very beneficial and greatly encouraging as I help them process through their wounded past at their own pace, respecting their free will and choice as the Lord does.

"We are coworkers belonging to God. You are God's field, God's building."

(1 CORINTHIANS 3:9, NET)

Since I began ministering Mind Renewing Healing Prayer, I have seen Jesus show up in ways that have totally shifted my understanding of emotional healing. God is so zealous to impart healing to us, His precious children, who have been wounded, broken and scarred by sin. It is His passion, as we see in Isaiah 61:1-3. Jesus paid the ultimate price, suffering and dying on the cross for our sins. He has given us a glorious salvation that not only includes forgiveness of our sins and eternal life, but also healing of the heart through the renewing of our minds. There is nothing greater for me than co-laboring with Jesus as He reveals His truth to us in our wounded memories and seeing the healing and resolution that only He can do.

The goal of entering into our healing journey is to experience true peace of mind and the revelation of our true identity as royal sons and daughters of the Most High God! This occurs during our healing journey as He imparts to us His truth that we are His children.

"…having predestined us to adoption as sons by Jesus Christ to Himself, according to the good pleasure of His will…"

(EPHESIANS 1:5, NKJV)

I firmly believe that the vast majority of Christians are hindered from moving forward in their calling and destiny because of varying degrees of lie-based beliefs anchored in our wounded past. If we will allow God to do the deep work of healing and mind renewal in the foundational memories of our past, we will walk in a far greater level of victory, liberty and breakthrough. I pray that this book opens your heart, touches you deeply, and encourages you to enter into your own personal healing journey.

CHAPTER 2

DECEIVED BY A LIE,
REMOVED FROM THE PRESENCE

"And they heard the sound of the Lord God walking in the garden in the cool of the day, and Adam and his wife hid themselves from the presence of the Lord God among the trees of the garden."
(GENESIS 3:8, NKJV)

HEALING PRINCIPLE: The enemy's ploy is to deceive us, as he did Adam and Eve. Ultimately, his goal is to cause us to remove ourselves from the presence of the Lord. Putting ourselves back in the Presence brings transformation: mind renewal uproots the lies planted by the enemy, and healing restores the posture of our heart.

I have read the Genesis account many times over the years, but I remember clearly the moment when I read Genesis 3:8 seemingly for the first time. Our church had recently conducted a 90-minute worship set during a service where the presence of the Lord fell so powerfully that the musicians stopped playing and the entire congregation worshiped the Lord in silence. In those moments, we bathed in His glory. Sensing that the Holy Spirit had moved in our midst, we recognized that our lives were powerfully touched; something had shifted, and we were not the same.

There is nothing like the presence of the Lord, and I am so honored to have found a community that prioritizes it. As I walk with God in my life's journey, I have learned that giving the presence of the Lord supreme authority and priority in my life has been a major key to breakthrough, especially as it relates to healing. I do not seek His presence solely to receive healing; I worship Him because He is worthy. Still, there is an undeniable and glorious direct correlation between His presence and our transformation.

It is of the utmost importance to learn to cultivate intimacy with the Lord in His presence. Adam and Eve knew this well. For many years, when I considered the Genesis account, I imagined that Adam and Eve walked daily with the Lord, until they sinned and hid themselves. But the first couple did more than just hide amongst the trees of the garden; they removed themselves from the very presence of the Lord and all of His glory.

Prior to Adam and Eve's disobedience, they had only experienced the presence of God. They knew nothing other than a Kingdom mindset. They did not have a broken, unhealthy childhood. They were not filled with lies from their past. In fact, they were filled with only good things and the word of God. Through conversing and walking with Him, they knew nothing apart from His awesome truth. Even so, Satan was able to twist the words of God in such a way that they were both deceived and subject to death.

God wants us to take His Word very seriously. In Genesis 2:16-17, the Lord gave Adam and Eve a simple, clear command. They had permission to live abundantly and eat of all the trees in the garden except for one. They were not to eat of the tree of the knowledge of good and evil under any circumstances or else their perfect, beautiful life would end and they would die. I assume they didn't understand what death was, but the command was clear regardless of their comprehension. God knew that eating of the tree would open a Pandora's box of sin, death, sickness, disease, strife, marital discord, rebellion, wars, and more. In His goodness, He desired to keep His children from evil.

Unlike Adam and Eve, humankind today is a byproduct of many generations and thousands of years of our descendants experiencing a sinful, fallen world. The enemy's ploy is to deceive us, as he did Adam and Eve, with lies, half-truths and distortions. His goal is to get us to choose to make bad choices that will compromise our walk with God, causing us to hide from His Presence. The moral of Adam and Eve's story is that if they can be deceived, how much more can you and I be led astray?

SATAN'S STRATEGY

Since the garden, Satan's goal has been to attack and sabotage the Word of God in order to undermine our true core identity, self-worth and destiny. If Satan's *goal* is to sabotage the Word of God in our lives, his *strategy* is to wound us early in our lives so that we might reject the Word. In doing so, Satan aims to limit our fruitfulness and keep us from our true destiny. He programs our minds by planting and reinforcing lies at an early age when we are most wounded, rejected, abandoned and abused.

When we are wounded, we are more likely to believe the lies we hear and make core foundational interpretations about our sense of worth, value and identity. Regardless of our logic, we live and react from the place of the lie. Satan knows that even when we are taught biblical truths, lies that we believe in the core of our being enable *internal dissonance*. That is, even when truth is layered on top of these foundational lie-based beliefs, we may still have difficulty laying hold of God's Word and promises for our lives. If we have difficulty embracing God's Word, then we will have difficulty walking in the fullness of our destiny, life purpose and calling.

GOD'S REMEDY

"...The reason the Son of God was made manifest (visible) was to undo (destroy, loosen, and dissolve) the works the devil [has done]."

(1 JOHN 1:8, AMP)

If Satan's goal is to undermine our ability to hear, understand and apply the Word of God in our lives, God's remedy is to restore our capacity to know Him, and ourselves, through His Word. This means that learning to walk in God's Word and in His promises is extremely important and relevant to our survival and triumph over evil. Thank God that He has given us the Holy Spirit as an inner teacher and counselor to guide us and to give witness to His Word!

I believe that God accomplishes His desire to restore His children through total healing. We can discern from the New Testament's use of the word *sozo* (literally: to save) that Jesus came not only to "save" us from our sin, but to heal and deliver His children. Just like the Stevie Wonder song "Signed, Sealed, Delivered—I'm Yours!" we can sing, "Saved, Healed, Delivered—We're His!"

In this eternal plan, God intended us to experience the renewing of our minds and the healing of our hearts. In His goodness, God made a plan through Jesus to ensure that "by His stripes we are healed."[1] Through the shedding of Jesus' blood on the cross, and by His resurrection, God's awesome eternal plan is to bring *sozo* to us, the heirs of this glorious salvation.

"My sheep hear My voice, and I know them, and they follow Me."

(JOHN 10:27, NKJV)

---

[1] Isaiah 53:5

Jesus came to undo, deliver us from and totally destroy the hold of Satan, the enemy of our souls. Jesus' heart is to bring us into right relationship with our loving heavenly Father. He has placed in our hands the weapons of warfare, which is His Word. If Satan tries to undermine God's Word, Jesus incarnates it so that it might be reestablished in our lives. Jesus makes it clear in the book of John that *"My sheep hear my voice."*[2] We not only have the capacity to hear God, but we can rest assured that God expects for us to hear His voice so that we might grow in intimacy with Him. God set the precedent for communication with Adam and Eve in the garden by walking and talking with them daily. Even now, God desires to communicate deeply with us, on a daily basis, that we might have rich relationship with Him.

> *"For the weapons of our warfare are not carnal, but mighty in God for pulling down strongholds, casting down arguments and every high thing that exalts itself against the knowledge of God, bringing every thought into captivity to the obedience of Christ."*
>
> (2 CORINTHIANS 10:4-5, NKJV)

Mind Renewing Healing Prayer is one way to connect and communicate with God. Based on the Word of God, a mighty weapon for pulling down strongholds, it is a powerful tool that, if done correctly, can result in tremendous healing, deliverance and breakthrough for those in need. When we enter into a Mind Renewing Healing Prayer session (more on this later), the goal is to co-labor with Christ in the healing process. I do this by helping people find their triggered emotional reactions. Then we help them go to the root memory containers where their lie-based beliefs have been planted, cultivated and reinforced throughout their lives. The bottom line is, Satan uses all his resources to undermine God's Word and the truth about our true identity. He wants to attack or hide God's goodness and His promises for our lives just as he did with Adam and Eve in the garden. Satan wants us to perceive things from his

---

[2] John 10:27

point of view to keep us limited, hindered and defeated throughout our lives. He is a master spin doctor. His goal is to remove us from the presence of God by disrupting our alignment with the Word of God. Though he may be effective at times, Satan does not have the final word.

> *So I will restore to you the years that the swarming locust has eaten…*
> *You shall eat in plenty and be satisfied,*
> *And praise the name of the Lord your God,*
> *Who has dealt wondrously with you;*
> *And My people shall never be put to shame.*
> *Then you shall know that I am in the midst of Israel:*
> *I am the Lord your God*
> *And there is no other.*
> *My people shall never be put to shame.*
>
> (JOEL 2:25-27, NKJV)

The good news is that, through the finished work of the cross, the Lord has given us a backup plan to renew our lie-based minds, heal our broken hearts, and restore the years the locust has stolen. Praise the Lord! This is the focus of the book before you. God has given us a plan to reveal the strongholds and lie-based thinking that life's circumstances and the enemy have planted in our hearts and minds. As we engage in the healing process, we become more and more capable of accepting and integrating His Word into our lives in real and practical ways.

In this book, I will help you identify the lies that have taken root in your life and teach you how to encounter the Lord's healing presence through the Holy Spirit. Through practical examples and personal testimonies, I will show you how to renew your mind through Spirit-led truth encounters and lead others into their own healing paths. Together, we will embark upon a journey that moves us from uprooting the strongholds and core beliefs that are wreaking havoc in our lives to walking in the wholeness that we all so deeply desire.

MY STORY

In Genesis, God allowed Satan, in the form of a serpent, to challenge Adam and Eve and to tempt them to dismiss the spoken word of God. Why would God permit that? This is a mystery that I plan to ask God when I get to heaven, but in any case, it's clear that God allows us to face the same temptations today. In the same way that Adam and Eve were deceived in the garden, I was deceived as a youth. I remember an onslaught of deceptive messages that flooded my young life by leading me away from the church and that caused me to turn into a wayward, rebellious teen. I was fourteen years old in 1967 when the counterculture exploded with drugs, free love and rock and roll. I watched with wonder the media coverage of the masses of hippies converging from around the nation to the Haight-Ashbury Section of San Francisco, the epicenter of this massive cultural rebellion, shift and explosion. I really wanted to leave home, go there and be a part of what was happening. I didn't go to San Francisco then, but the counterculture spread like wildfire across America, and soon even our little town in Ohio was steeped in drugs and a countercultural subculture. All over the world, the young and rebellious were seduced by the "father of lies" with very appealing images of the apparent freedom that sex, drugs, alcohol and rock and roll seemed to offer. The promises of a life without responsibility or consequences for our sinful choices proved very tempting. Many of us chased after a lifestyle that promised peace, love and Nirvana. A couple of years later, in 1969, the unprecedented Woodstock rock festival happened. Hundreds of thousands of young people invaded a small town in upstate New York for three days of drugs, sex and rock and roll. The event reinforced these same lies to millions of impressionable adolescents. I, along with many of my Baby Boomer peers, were led astray from our Christian roots into massive deception, which included free love, substance abuse, eastern religious experiences and mysticism. Millions were led into confusion and destruction in the wake of what proved to be a mass media deception. These images were reinforced by our rock and roll heroes, who, in retrospect were as clueless as we were. Little did I know, my life was almost destroyed for a season because of many poor life choices and a season of massive drug and alcohol abuse. Although many of my generation were enamored by the counterculture of the '60s and '70s, it was extremely easy for those of us who were hurt and broken to drown and medicate our pain without even knowing that's what we were doing. Thanks to the prayers of many, and especially a powerful interceding mother, I had a dramatic conversion to Christ at nineteen years of age. That encounter changed the course of my life; it marked the beginning of my healing journey as well as the renewal of my mind.

> *"But even if our gospel is veiled, it is veiled to those who are perishing, whose minds the god of this age has blinded, who do not believe, lest the light of the gospel of the glory of Christ, who is the image of God, should shine on them."*
>
> (2 CORINTHIANS 4:3-4, NKJV)

The objects of our personal temptations are often beautiful, pleasant to the eyes, and desirable to our flesh. Satan's strategy is the same today as it was with Adam and Eve. Any parent knows that we tell our children and warn them of the dangers that they may face in life because we care for them. Far too often they disregard our advice and the warnings we give and end up making poor life decisions. Unfortunately, humankind often responds to our heavenly Father in the same manner. We in the Woodstock generation rebelled against the Word of God just as Lucifer and his fallen angels did in heaven. We fell prey to the same deception that Adam and Eve fell prey to in the garden of Eden. Far too many of us thought we knew better than our parents and, ultimately, God Himself; we believed that we could chart our own destiny apart from Him. As everyone ultimately does, I found out that rebellion always ends badly.

> *"And the Lord God commanded the man, saying, 'Of every tree of the garden you may freely eat; but of the tree of the knowledge of good and evil you shall not eat, for in the day*

that you eat of it you shall surely die."

(GENESIS 2:16-17, NKJV)

If we want to walk in victory and overcome all that keeps us from wholeness, I believe there is an important revelation we must grasp: *God did not tell Adam and Eve much about the tree from which they were not to eat; instead, God told them all they needed to know to live abundantly, thrive and overcome.* In my experience, I have found that God does the same thing for us today. If we will listen to God, He will reveal to us all we need to know in order to thrive and overcome. We are incapable of fully understanding all there is to know about God, the world and His kingdom. In obstinance or pride, we often resist our heavenly Father because of the things that we cannot understand. However, walking in a greater measure of His revelation is a beautiful thing. In writing this book, the Lord has blessed me with new revelation and a greater understanding of who He is and who we are in Him. However, one of the keys to victory is to continue tuning into His Word and, by faith, accepting what we do not know and cannot understand.

"For My thoughts are not your thoughts,
Nor are your ways My ways," says the Lord.
For as the heavens are higher than the earth,
So are My ways higher than your ways,
And My thoughts than your thoughts.

(ISAIAH 55:8-9, NKJV)

God does not think like we think, and His ways are not our ways. We must learn to seek, live in and treasure dwelling in His Presence. We must develop the spiritual disciplines of meditating upon His Word. We must lean into Him, allowing Him to bring us up into a higher Kingdom plane and perspective. We must not allow ourselves to dwell and live in a carnal, earthly mindset. The only way to overcome the flesh is to walk in the Spirit and Presence of God.

"You will show me the path of life;

In Your presence is fullness of joy;
At Your right hand are pleasures forevermore."

(PSALM 16:11, NKJV)

Can you imagine the fullness of joy Adam and Eve must have experienced as they walked daily in His Presence? Can you imagine the intimacy of walking and communing with Him in the garden? How awesome that must have been! When we understand the power of His presence, we begin to comprehend what Adam and Eve lost when they were deceived in the garden. Their deception led them to flee the powerful, life-giving force that is His presence.

Today, I understand the significance of Scripture far more than ever before. I have grown over the years in experiencing the Holy Spirit and know how rich it is to dwell in His Presence. I love and so appreciate it today because throughout my earlier life I had not always known, valued or experienced God's Presence personally. Knowing *about* it and experiencing it are two entirely different things.

When you know the Presence of the Lord, you understand the gravity of what it means to lose it. You also know that it's worth forsaking all other things to find the only solution to our fragile, broken human condition. Healing and breakthrough happen as a byproduct of encountering God's Presence and from having a fresh revelation of the truth of His Word. Mind Renewing Healing Prayer is one vehicle through which the broken can encounter the Presence; it is a tool that helps one hear, through the Holy Spirit, the voice of Jesus as He speaks directly to the lies and brokenness in our hearts and minds.

The remainder of this book will establish how lie-based belief systems are planted and evolve in the mind. I will also address how mental strongholds develop and how our defense mechanisms can hinder our healing process. I will also illustrate how Mind Renewing Healing Prayer helps us navigate the healing process.

CHAPTER 3

TURNING YOUR HEART OF STONE TO A HEART OF FLESH

"I will give you a new heart and put a new spirit in you; I will remove from you your heart of stone and give you a heart of flesh. And I will put my Spirit in you and move you to follow my decrees and be careful to keep my laws."
(EZEKIEL 36:26-27, NIV)

HEALING PRINCIPLE: God created us with defense mechanisms to help us survive life's traumas and tragedies. These defense mechanisms help us survive but prevent us from thriving when used inappropriately. When we continuously operate out of our defense mechanisms, instead of receiving the Lord's healing, we run the risk of developing a heart of stone. God's heart is to bring total healing to our hearts, to turn them from stone to flesh.

The first order of business in pursuing our healing journey is to realize that we all have psychological defense mechanisms; in fact, we are created with them. Defense mechanisms help us to deal with life in times of trial, adversity, trauma and abuse. They also help us survive combat in times of war, accidents of various sorts, and difficult life situations in childhood and adulthood. Defense mechanisms are not negative; God created us with the capacity to utilize them and help us survive overwhelming circumstances. However, when we operate out of our defense mechanisms for prolonged periods of time without working through our emotional pain, they can hinder our healing, growth and development.

Most of us are familiar with defense mechanisms. In response to emotional or psychological pain, many of us build internal walls or fortresses to guard our hearts and minds. We do this subconsciously as a way to cope and, ultimately, to survive. However, when we do this repeatedly, our hearts and minds begin to shut down, and we start to operate in denial and suppression. This causes our *lie-based core beliefs* to remain intact. When this becomes a lifestyle, we end up living a diminished existence. As we remain shut down for prolonged periods of time, be it weeks, months or years, a heart a stone begins to emerge. In the same way that clogged arteries prevent blood flow in the physical heart, a heart of stone stops healthy emotional and spiritual life flow. When used inappropriately, defense mechanisms create a heart posture that inhibits us from connecting with God, receiving His healing, and living abundantly.

We see the first evidence of defense mechanisms in the Garden of Eden.

REMOVED FROM THE PRESENCE

> *Then the man said, "The woman whom You gave to be with me, she gave me of the tree, and I ate." And the Lord God said to the woman, "What is this you have done?"*
>
> *The woman said, "The serpent deceived me, and I ate."*
>
> (GENESIS 3:12-13, NKJV)

After they sinned and ate the fruit from the forbidden tree, Adam and Eve's defense mechanisms kicked in, causing them to hide, cover their nakedness, and self-defend. They removed themselves from the Presence of the Lord. They misappropriated their defense mechanisms by projecting blame and avoiding personal responsibility. When Adam blamed God and Eve in Genesis 3:12, and Eve shifted fault to the serpent in verse 13, they distorted the defense mechanisms God had given them for inappropriate use: to cover their sin and pain. This has been a major coping mechanism of mankind ever since.

Did you ever stop to think that Adam and Eve did not have a wounded, broken, dysfunctional childhood? Their actions were not a result of bad parenting. They were loved, nurtured and taught directly by the living God from the beginning. Even in ideal circumstances, sinful human nature defends, projects and avoids responsibility. This is magnified when we have been raised in broken homes and dysfunctional environments.

We all grow up in a fallen world and, as a result, we all utilize defense mechanisms to navigate difficult experiences and protect ourselves from pain. For instance, when we experience the death of a loved one, defenses help us cope with the tragedy. Denial helps us to cope with the grief initially until we can, step by step, completely integrate the loss of a loved one into our daily experience. Denial helps us deal with the accompanying feelings of depression, sadness, fear and anger until we can more effectively process and release them. Those who have experienced trauma in extremely severe forms, for example a victim of sexual molestation or a soldier who has experienced life-threatening combat, may suppress and compartmentalize the experience to prevent complete breakdown. They may even bury, repress or dissociate some or all parts of their memories. Ideally, this is done *until* they can allow their painful thoughts, emotions and physical memories to surface. It also helps them better deal with the smells, tastes and sounds of a traumatic event *until* they are better equipped to process its intensity. At its best, life can be extremely painful, and defense mechanisms are meant to help us *temporarily* survive emotionally difficult times.

"Then they cried out to the Lord in their trouble, and He saved them out of their distresses. He sent His word and healed them, and delivered them from their destructions."

(PSALM 107:19-20, NKJV)

While the Lord created defenses for our good, He did not intend for us to remain in them indefinitely. Ultimately, His desire is to heal our hearts. Unfortunately, many of us are so emotionally defended that we are often unaware of the extent of our need for healing and restoration. In these instances, prolonged denial of a need for healing creates an environment where the heart becomes hardened and shuts down. In other words, what helped the person get through difficulty now prevents them from opening to the Lord to receive His healing.

Many of us come into God's kingdom wounded, bruised and broken, but it is not God's heart that we remain this way. As we welcome Christ in our hearts as our personal Savior, He plants a seed of hope within us. This seed is the reminder that He has provided for our healing, deliverance, mind renewal and restoration.

NOT SURVIVING, BUT THRIVING

"The thief does not come except to steal, and to kill, and to destroy. I have come that they may have life, and that they may have it more abundantly."

(JOHN 10:10, NKJV)

The Lord's will for us is to have an abundant life, to thrive by centering ourselves in Him and by receiving the healing that only God can give. His desire is that we allow Him to give us a new heart, renew our mind and put His spirit in us. He wants to remove our hearts of stone and replace them with hearts of flesh (see Ezekiel 36:26). Mind Renewing Healing Prayer is a tool the Lord has given me to help believers proactively seek His healing by breaking down the barriers around our hearts and minds that keep us in bondage. This process allows all of us, myself included, to begin to work through our protective defenses.

As a healing prayer minister and therapist, I have many people come to my office seeking help. Our defenses often operate below the level of conscious awareness. The alcoholic in denial is often unaware of his condition and may claim, "I don't have a drinking problem; I can stop whenever I want," despite multiple DUIs and his wife's decision to leave him. The woman in a marital conflict may project her anger onto her husband, screaming at him while making the accusation he is "angry at her." People are continually surprised at the memories and lie-based beliefs that underlie emotionally triggered reactions to daily situations. (More on triggers in chapter 6.) Mind Renewing Healing Prayer helps us work through these triggers and defenses so that, as walls come down, we may enter into the places in our memories where lie-based beliefs are buried. I never cease to be amazed as Jesus, through the Holy Spirit, brings His truth and light into the wounded areas of the heart and mind so that His people can experience peace, release and breakthrough.

OVERCOMING STRONGHOLDS

"Therefore if the Son makes you free, you shall be free indeed."

(JOHN 8:36, NKJV)

The mind builds defenses when our hearts are wounded. We have all been hurt to some degree, but the development of mental *strongholds* occur when we are wounded in childhood. In moments of brokenness, we make internal interpretations of negative life events. For example, the childhood sexual abuse victim may feel that the abuse was their fault or that they are "bad" or "dirty" because of what happened. What takes precedence in the mind of the child is what is believed in *memory* more than the objective reality of the situation. In other words, the child's *interpretation* of an event takes precedence over the truth. As a result, the child internalizes core lie-based beliefs and faulty thinking emerges. This is the foundation for a stronghold to take root.

A *stronghold* is any belief that is not in line with God's Word and objective reality. Satan's strategy is to plant lies in our minds during our childhood that develop into strongholds that will last into and throughout adulthood. A stronghold develops when internal interpretations of negative life events become core beliefs. For example, when a person who has been sexually molested as a child begins to view the situation as their fault, a stronghold has been established in the mind of the child. If the stronghold is not deconstructed, it will become the interpretive lens through which the child views himself and the world around him for the remainder of his life. While the adult who has experienced childhood trauma may rationally know the truth (i.e., the abuse was not their fault), the stronghold may keep them from experiencing true freedom. This is, in part, due to the way the mind functions.

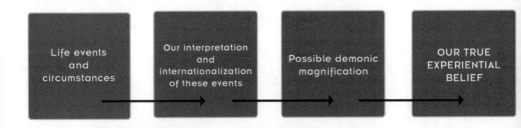

There are two parts of the mind: the *rational room* and the *experiential room*.[1] The first room is where facts, knowledge and data help us reason. In this part of the mind, logic governs. The reason that I can intellectually know the truth about something, but not experience freedom in this area, is that core beliefs are stored in another part of the mind: the experiential room.

The experiential room is the subconscious part of the mind

---

[1] This is a Theophostic concept from Dr. Ed Smith.

and the place where memories, and our interpretations of those memories, are stored. Our memories and interpretations of past experiences create our core beliefs, which are more potent than the objective truth of the event. Our triggered emotional self reacts daily from this part of the mind. This is why a childhood abuse victim may logically know his abuse was not his fault but might still walk through life feeling "bad, dirty and ashamed" on a daily basis. This is how a stronghold evolves to corrupt an entire belief system.

The crux of the matter is that while we can know the truth about something, we can still remain in bondage. The main point of this book is to demonstrate that it is possible to allow the Lord to reveal His truth to the lies still residing in the core memories of our wounded past and experience true freedom. Since we all live and daily react from the experiential room, we *all* need to learn how to let Jesus bring us breakthrough in this area.

Because the mind builds defenses when the heart is wounded, the work of healing necessarily begins with bringing down these walls. Proverbs 23:7 says, "For as he thinks in his heart, so is he." Mind renewal is critical to heart healing.

DEVELOPING A HARDENED HEART

> *"While it is said: 'Today, if you will hear His voice, Do not harden your hearts as in the rebellion.'"*
>
> (HEBREWS 3:15, NKJV)

A heart becomes hardened when we *experience* brokenness, but it *stays* hardened because of the choices we make. While strongholds originate in childhood, we often make decisions throughout adult-hood that reinforce those strongholds, keeping our hearts of stone intact. For example, we may make vows, or defensive decisions to emotionally self-protect, that shut down and disconnect our hearts. Or we may make conscious decisions to engage in sinful lifestyle choices by remaining unrepentant and ignoring our need to address sin. Vows are the building material for hearts of stone and sinful lifestyle choices to evolve into unhealthy patterns of dealing with hurt. Both fortify strongholds and prevent us from receiving total heart healing.

RESULTS OF A HARDENED HEART

".... Today, after such a long time, as it has been said:
Today, if you will hear His voice, Do not harden your hearts."

(HEBREWS 4:7, NKJV)

A hardened heart may result in addiction, relational disconnect or derailment from God's divine purpose in your life. A hardened heart may cause us to use mood altering addictive and avoidant behavior to numb pain or may encourage us to isolate ourselves from relationships that could *potentially* cause us pain. If we allow ourselves to be governed by our hearts of stone, we run the risk of becoming increasingly ineffective in our ministry, calling or life purpose. Those who are already in ministry run the risk of being hindered or derailed if they do not pursue their own healing journey. The enemy of our souls has painted a bullseye squarely on our wounded heart with lie-based beliefs. The first step toward healing is to deal with your hardened heart of stone. If you choose not to deal with your heart of stone, you will not be able to walk in the fullness of God's intention for your life.

Many things may prevent us from dealing with a heart of stone (fear, false teaching, pride or being well-defended). A heart that has repeatedly ignored the Holy Spirit's wooing over time may further desensitize to the point where a heart of stone emerges. For some of you reading this book, it has been *such a long time.* Like many I see in my practice, some of you have covered, isolated and defended yourself for months, years or even decades. If you recognize your own patterns of burial, suppression and denial as you read this, know that today can be a new beginning! Scripture affirms that *if you hear His voice*, He will turn your heart of stone to a heart of flesh.

DEALING WITH YOUR HARDENED HEART

> *"Therefore, confess your sins to one another, and pray for one another so that you may be healed. The effective prayer of a righteous man can accomplish much."*
>
> (JAMES 5:16, NASB)

The resulting curse of sin was for Adam to labor in tilling the soil to produce a fruitful harvest and for Eve to experience pain in childbirth. In the same way, we must till the soil of our minds by removing the thorns and entanglements around our minds and prepare the ground of our heart by removing the rocks and stony places. We may experience pain in the process of working through our past, but as we ask the Lord to lead us in the process of tending the garden of our soul, we will move steadily toward healing and restoration. Because of the Father's love for us, He has provided an open door for our healing through the death and resurrection of Jesus—by His stripes we are healed! We only need to be willing to receive the fullness of His sacrifice for us. As we allow Him to work in and through us, the cultivation of our hearts will birth our divine life purpose and destiny.

Do you desire that the Lord would turn your heart of stone into a heart of flesh? Begin the process of dealing with your hardened heart right now with the steps and prayer outlined below.

1. **Repent.** Your healing journey begins with repentance. Begin by asking Him to turn your heart of stone to a heart of flesh.

2. **Deal with past offenses**. Repent from your heart and confess them to the Lord and to another believer.

3. **Be honest with yourself** and accountable to others. Find a trustworthy Christian of the same sex with whom to share your struggles, temptations and areas of brokenness; pray for one another.

4. **Choose** to take whatever steps are necessary to enter into and fully engage in your healing journey.

Prayer:

Lord, I repent of any sins that I have committed that have hindered my walk with You. (Name your sin.)

I know the the wounds of my past are not my fault, but, Lord, I repent of controlling and managing my pain myself. I thank You for creating me with defense mechanisms that helped me to survive. However, I repent from the ways I have knowingly or unknowingly used them longer than they were ever intended. (Name and repent of those defenses.)

I choose instead to let You be my defense and my strong tower. I repent for any ways I have managed my pain with addictive, mood altering addictive behaviors, (name addictive behaviors) instead of trusting You with my life, my pain, my hurt and my future. I ask You to help me today to begin the process of turning my heart of stone to a heart of flesh. I ask You to help me to fully engage my heart and mind on my healing journey. I ask that You would provide the people, resources, as well as the desire and will to walk in the full measure of healing, wholeness and mind renewal that You intend for me.

Amen.

CHAPTER 4

RENEWING THE MIND

"For as he thinks in his heart, so is he."
PROVERBS 23:7 (NKJV)

HEALING PRINCIPLE: The consequence of sin is that our mental hard drives have been compromised and corrupted. As a result, we are filled with lie-based beliefs in the core of our being. Everything we do is rooted in what we believe. God wants to renew our minds to transform our whole lives—not just our beliefs, but our actions as well.

Make no mistake that sin is the core problem of humankind; it is why we are in need of a Savior. When man sinned, his communion with God was drastically altered and he was removed from the Presence he enjoyed in the garden. Among other things, abuse, abandonment, shame, unworthiness, low self-esteem, depression, fear, anxiety and various mental disorders entered the world and man slowly started to die. The emotional and mental consequences of sin for humanity were brokenness, emotional pain and suffering. At the root of it all, lies and mental strongholds became deeply entrenched in the heart and mind of man. Like a virus, sin corrupted our mental hard drives, impacting all our beliefs, decisions and actions.

The enemy of our souls knows that our core belief system is the *foundation* of all we think, believe and ultimately do. He works hard to attack our minds in our formative years in order to corrupt both our mindset as well as our core memories. Our core memories are formative and determine how we perceive ourselves and the world. Unfortunately, in humanity's fallen state, we all filter our decisions and choices through a corrupted lens that distorts who we are and who God is. Because our belief system is foundational to how we perceive ourselves, God and the world around us, reprogramming our hard drive requires us to return to the source of all truth: God's Word.

> *"Therefore whoever hears these sayings of Mine, and does them, I will liken him to a wise man who built his house on the rock: and the rain descended, the floods came, and the winds blew and beat on that house; and it did not fall, for it was founded on the rock. But everyone who hears these sayings of Mine, and does not do them, will be like a foolish man who built his house on the sand: and the rain descended, the floods came, and the winds blew and beat on that house; and it fell. And great was its fall."*
>
> (MATTHEW 7:24-27, NKJV)

Scripture says that in order to build a great house, we must choose a great foundation upon which to construct it. If we understand that God's Word is the basis of all truth and revelation for mankind, we will use it to discover Jesus as the foundation upon which to build our lives.

Many of us are familiar with the passage of the house upon the rock, but few understand what it means to construct our lives on a foundation of truth. That is to say, if our core mindset is based on beliefs of unworthiness, fear, shame and self-contempt, we will never have the sturdy foundation God desires for us. Instead, we will struggle to lay hold of the abundant, overcoming life He died to give us. If we build our lives on sand, the storms of life will ultimately knock us down. In the same way, if the core foundational beliefs of our minds are filled with lie-based thinking and beliefs, we will never walk in the fullness the Lord intends for our lives. We only get one shot at life. We must make the most of the gift of life that the Lord has granted to each one of us by recognizing what He has made available to us.

SCRIPTURE AND MIND RENEWAL

The foundation of truth, and our standard for right thinking, is the revealed Word of God. The Word of God is His revelation to mankind—His road map showing the way to a victorious, rich and abundant life with God. Satan's strategy is subtle; instead of attacking the Word of God directly, he tries to distort our mindsets, including how we perceive God's Word. To guard against these attacks, we must take hold of the Word of God as the foundation of all our thinking.

Many pose the questions, if the Word of God is the foundation that establishes our correct way of thinking, why do we need mind renewal? Isn't the Word of God enough to guide and direct our lives? Absolutely, it is. The Bible clearly renews our mind daily as we meditate and contemplate His Word. So why the need for mind renewal? To me, it is not a matter of whether or not the Word of

God is enough, but it is a question of how we apply the Word in our lives and whether or not it leads us to an encounter where we can hear the voice of God. The Bible teaches us that "My sheep hear My voice, and I know them, and they follow Me" (John 10:27, NKJV). Scripture is one way we hear His voice, but there are other ways we can hear His voice.

In my work as a clinical social worker in a private counseling practice, I have spent thousands of hours working with people who have experienced brokenness, oppression and wounds. In my experience, wounds come from three different sources. Sometimes, *psychological* wounds come from relational conflicts. These may manifest in marital problems, parent-child conflicts, poor parenting, and poor interpersonal skills. Many times, individuals who experience difficulty with interpersonal relationships cause problems not only in the family, but in the workplace, community and church as well. A small percentage of these individuals are so troubled with psychological and interpersonal relationship problems, their triggered emotional reactions place an unnecessary burden on church or community leaders. Relational issues manifest in different ways, but it is common for those who have relational issues to struggle with establishing or maintaining proper boundaries. This may make them highly dependent on others or cause them to take on unhealthy caretaking roles. These people need our love, guidance, support and the Lord's healing touch.

Then there are others who suffer with *chemical imbalance*. Some Christians misunderstand that there *are* some issues that are *physiological* in nature. They may struggle with severe depression, anxiety, panic attacks, obsessive compulsive disorder, psychosis, bipolar disorder and other psychological disorders. Most of us could benefit from Mind Renewing Healing Prayer and counseling from time to time. The exception, in my opinion, is when someone is psychotic, delusional, hearing voices, hallucinating or paranoid. These people need to be treated with psychotropic medications in the same way that a diabetic needs insulin to help stabilize their medical condition. That is *not* to say we should cease praying for the physical and emotional healing of these individuals. In fact, it is biblical and essential that we pray for all who are sick with various illnesses. But there are cases when medical intervention is necessary to provide the body with immediate stability so the person can begin their healing journey.

In this category, along with those who are actively psychotic are those who struggle with suicidal tendencies and those who are dissociated. Some Christians do not have a clear understanding of these issues and wrongly believe that all people need is deliverance from the demonic. Dissociation is a psychological effect that takes place when a person's mind has fragmented due to early childhood abuse or trauma. I have encountered many individuals whose dissociation has been misunderstood as demonization. In addition to this being extremely hurtful to the person experiencing dissociation, incorrectly identifying the problem prevents the individual from receiving the healing they desperately need. In my ministry, I have heard many stories of those who have been misunderstood as demonized, when, in reality, an angry, protective part of their fragmented self was emerging. That is not to say that a dissociated person cannot be demonized. Rather, this is to say that when we minister Mind Renewal Healing Prayer we must remember that psychological and psychiatric problems are real and do present in prayer sessions. While I would still pray for the healing of these individuals, they may benefit from seeing a physician or psychiatrist for a consultation to determine if medication is required.[1]

Just as some issues are primarily physiological, some issues are predominantly *spiritual* in their origins. That is to say, they are demonic in nature. This is the third category of issues that present among those seeking emotional healing. Of course there are also times when a person presents a problem that is a combination of psychological (lie-based), physiological and spiritual. This is where wisdom and discernment are of the utmost importance.

Whether an individual's problems are psychological, physio-

---

[1] If you are a lay minister and find that someone is suicidal, I urge you to minister Mind Renewing Healing Prayer only in cases when the individual is under the care or supervision of a mental health professional, and when you are under the authority of your church's prayer ministry team. Failure to exercise wisdom in this case is to put the person you are ministering to and yourself at risk.

logical or demonic at the root, the presentation is often the same: depression, anxiety, panic, low self-esteem and other emotional issues. Those who are wounded and traumatized often believe that they are worthless, unloved and unwanted. In my ministry, I have learned the power of the Word of God, whether it comes through applying Scripture or by leading someone into an encounter with the Holy Spirit. Sometimes, it is only the Word of God that can provide the healing needed to confirm and reestablish a sense of worth, love and belonging. This is the basis of Mind Renewing Healing Prayer and the subject to which we will now turn our attention.

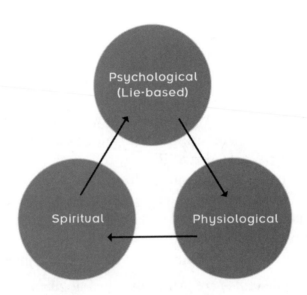

INTRODUCTION TO MIND RENEWING HEALING PRAYER

One of the ways the Theophostic and Mind Renewing Healing Prayer methods differ from other approaches is its focus on the healing of hurts, past wounds and traumatic memories, particularly foundational childhood memories. Everyone has memories, but depending on our childhood experiences we may experience memories that are more or less traumatic than others. In psychological terms, the *memory* is the container of a historical event that stores an interpretation that the person made during the event. Because children are narcissistic and egocentric by nature, deep wounds, hurt and trauma generally cause them to make a distorted interpretation, during which time a *lie* is formed. For example, if a child repeatedly sees his or her parents arguing about parenthood, and their fighting results in a divorce, the child may interpret the divorce as being their fault. Similarly, if a child is physically, emotional or sexually abused, they may interpret the experience with feelings of guilt or shame; despite their experience, they may interpret the event as their fault, even throughout adulthood. Through the interpretations of memories like these, lies internalize into a child's psyche. Through emotional triggers, they are reinforced throughout the child's life. The work of Mind Renewing Healing Prayer is to uproot these lies and bring healing to the memories and triggered reactions they cause in the person's life.

THE ROOMS OF THE MIND

The key to understanding how to uproot lies and bring healing to memories is to understand how the mind works. With just a few foundational concepts, inner healing can become less complicated and confusing. Taking the example above, there are times when a person may *intellectually* understand that their childhood abuse was not their fault but may not be able to let go of the feelings of guilt associated with that experience. This is a common occurrence because of how childhood memories are formed and how the mind operates.

In order to better understand how Mind Renewing Healing Prayer can play a role in the healing of memories, it is helpful to consider the following illustration. Imagine, if you will, that the mind has two rooms: one is the *logical room* and the other is the *experiential room*. The logical room is the place of reason. In it, we find rational facts, knowledge and data. This part of our mind helps us know and understand truth on an intellectual level. For instance, the logical room helps me to make sense of the idea that

"I am fearfully and wonderfully made" (Psalm 139:14, EVS), even when I don't feel like it is my reality.

The other part of the mind is the *experiential room*. This is where past memory events are stored. It's also the place where we make interpretations of these past events. In this room, emotional reactions surface from these interpretations, exposing our true core beliefs. For those who have experienced hurt, wounds or trauma, this is both the place where emotional pain is stored and the place from which triggers emerge. If we know the Lord but have experienced emotional trauma in our past, we may embrace Psalm 139 in the *logical room* but keep it from entering our *experiential room*.

The goal of emotional healing is to break through the defenses, identity lie-based beliefs in core foundational memories, ask Jesus to reveal truth and thus strengthen the pathway between the logical and experiential rooms in our mind. The key to this breakthrough is to answer the question "How do we access our lie-based beliefs and receive a revelation of truth in the experiential part of our mind?" The purpose of this book is to answer this question with a theoretical explanation accompanied by practical, real-life examples based on my experiences in ministry. It is to this topic that we now turn our attention.

PART TWO

PREPARING FOR MIND RENEWING HEALING PRAYER

CHAPTER 5

THE HEART OF THE MATTER

"Indeed, we put bits in horses' mouths that they may obey us, and we turn their whole body. Look also at ships: although they are so large and are driven by fierce winds, they are turned by a very small rudder wherever the pilot desires. Even so the tongue is a little member and boasts great things. See how great a forest a little fire kindles! And the tongue is a fire, a world of iniquity. The tongue is so set among our members that it defiles the whole body, and sets on fire the course of nature; and it is set on fire by hell."
(JAMES 3:3-6, NKJV)

HEALING PRINCIPLE: In order to be effective in the healing ministry, we must determine to deeply explore and genuinely deal with our own issues. We must be willing to process through our broken places, identify our core lie-based beliefs rooted in past foundational memories, and pursue our own healing journey. In order to have true change, we must not only ask God to help us deal with our shortcomings and brokenness; we must turn over the fallow ground of our hearts and ask God to make us ready and willing to press into freedom, healing and divine breakthrough.

All that has been said previously in this book lays a foundation for the principles of Mind Renewing Healing Prayer. The process behind Mind Renewing Healing Prayer is the heart of the matter, the core of the healing process. In the first part of this book, I laid out a foundation for why humanity is in need of emotional healing and why Jesus is the way, the truth and the life that leads to our complete wholeness. In the second part of this book, I will discuss how the prayer process works practically in a session between a prayer minister and a prayer recipient. The prayer process is easy to follow and simple to understand. At the same time, its impact can be powerful, far-reaching and life-changing.

Jason's Story

Jason was a 30-year-old male who came to see me, who was struggling with depression, grief and anxiety. As a teen, he had gotten in trouble with the law for some vandalism and spent a short time in jail. He learned a valuable life lesson and, since that time, had become a driven, hard-working young man, who lived with his girlfriend and their two young children. Jason was in the midst of a spiritual awakening following the death of his grandmother who had been a motherly figure and the sole stable figure in his life. He found her body and then had to help the paramedic put her in a body bag. He was having PTSD symptoms as he couldn't get these images of his grandmother's dead body and putting her into the body bag out of his mind.

At work, Jason, a heavy-equipment operator, was overly responsible; he couldn't say no to tasks. He was overwhelmed, distressed and experiencing anger outbursts. He was desperate for a breakthrough and open to our Mind Renewing Healing Prayer sessions. As we began to pray, he was triggered, feeling abandonment, disappointment, shame, and tightness in his chest. He immediately dropped into a memory of being arrested in his home and his mother's look of disbelief and disappointment as the police took him away. His lie-based beliefs, "I had let her down," and "I'm responsible for the younger kids," as well as the "fear of getting in trouble," filled this memory.

Jason was given a parental role as a child and was made to feel he was responsible for his mom after his dad abandoned him and his younger siblings. His mom left him with several younger siblings, and his grandmother, even though stern, provided his only sense of stability. As we processed through his past memories and as he gave Jesus his anger and rage, the Lord took it from him, along with his self-hatred. The Lord communicated to Jason, "That was in the past; it is over now. Let it go." The Lord also communicated to him that his siblings weren't his responsibility. Peace and calm not only filled the memory but uploaded to his life today. He had been continually frustrated at work when things weren't done correctly, usually by the other employees who he wasn't responsible for. His pattern throughout life of needing to take care of his siblings became a life pattern that left Jason feeling overwhelmed and overly responsible for many things in life that weren't his responsibility. This resulted in continual, compulsive working for his family, which caused him to be absent from the very ones he loved.

In the next session, we went to the memory where Jason's dad had left his mom. A few years later, during a conflict with his mom, sixteen-year-old Jason expressed a desire to live with his dad. In a fit of anger, his mother told him, "Your dad never wanted you; he wanted to abort you and wished you were never born." His mother spoke and reinforced a curse that his dad had already spoken in the past. Jason felt devastated, hurt, rejected, angry and confused by his mother's words.

> *"Death and life are in the power of the tongue, and they who indulge in it shall eat the fruit of it [for death or life]."*
>
> (PROVERBS 18:21, AMPC)

His mother and father spoke the worst type of curse, one that speaks literal death, instead of the words of life and blessing that God intends for parents to speak and communicate to their precious children! In response, Jason internalized lies that he was insignificant, of no value and didn't deserve to live. Out of this terrible psychological wounding and rejection, Jason made vows in agreement with the curses and lies. He made a vow that "I will do everything I can to prove him wrong." At 16 he quit high school and got a job full time and worked very hard day and night to prove "I'm worth keeping."

Great healing took place in Jason's life as we processed through this terrible memory and invited the Lord to communicate truth to it. I led Jason in a prayer to release his anger and rage toward his parents and in renouncing the curses made against him and the vows he made in response. Jesus revealed to Jason His truth "It was Dad's mistake, not mine." Jesus embraced him in the memory, communicating to him that he was wanted by Jesus and that "Jason would be a better dad to his children." Jason's countenance lit up; peace and calm enveloped him as he was engulfed in the heavenly Father's love.

His quality of life improved; he was much less angry at work and was soon spending more time with his kids. His relationship with his girlfriend improved and they decided to marry. Perhaps most importantly, he wasn't feeling a need to be in control of things that were not his responsibility any longer.

CO-LABORING WITH GOD

> *"Then they came to Him, bringing a paralytic who was carried by four men. And when they could not come near Him because of the crowd, they uncovered the roof where He was. So when they had broken through, they let down the bed on which the paralytic was lying."*
>
> (MARK 2:3-4, NKJV)

My experience is that nothing in life is more gratifying than co-laboring with God, so it is our great privilege to work alongside Him. Dr. Ed Smith uses the story of the paralytic to explain our role in facilitating and co-laboring with God. Our job, he says, is to metaphorically cut a hole in the roof and bring the wounded person before the Lord in their memory. We accomplish this by giving them permission to tap into their feelings, identify their false, lie-based beliefs and, through interceding, ask on their behalf for the Lord to reveal His truth to them. Just like the friends who lowered the paralytic to Jesus, we get to co-labor with Jesus, the healer of the brokenhearted, as we minister Mind Renewing Healing Prayer.

That being said, this kind of ministry is not for everyone, and training is essential. In my early years of ministry, I made many trips to conferences for training and honed my skills in the Basic and Advanced Theophostic principles. Similar to growing in the prophetic, we must observe experienced healing prayer ministers in order to digest the ministry *process* as well as the principles. Then we need to practice, practice, practice. At the point of writing this in 2015, I have personally facilitated more than 20,000 hours of Mind Renewing Healing Prayer. Like anything else we master and do well, it needs to become second nature. I cannot stress this enough. I have seen many people complete the training but fail to practice, learn and cultivate this process, which dramatically hinders their results in ministry.[1]

As with anything else in life, you will run into many obstacles when you begin your healing ministry. In the same way that a young surgeon who recently graduated medical school may be able to complete some routine surgeries fairly well, beginning your training in Mind Renewing Healing Prayer principles will help you as you begin your ministry work. But if you want to develop the skill and mastery to deal with the more complex situations, it will take years of practice, training and cultivation. Not everyone is called or cut out for inner healing ministry. However, training combined with practice will mature and prepare you to handle the unique challenges that come with it.

---

[1] In the future, I hope to publish my own Mind Renewing Healing Prayer training manual for those who want to pursue training in this ministry.

YOUR HEALING JOURNEY

As you seek training opportunities, it is critical that you pursue your own healing as well. We all need healing. It is common for people who have experienced deep wounds to be drawn to learn and administer Mind Renewing Healing Prayer. However, some are not yet ready to facilitate the process and need first to receive. Otherwise, these people are at risk of reinforcing their unhealthy patterns of caretaking and drawing their sense of worth from their benevolent behavior. Because they are naturally other-oriented, their actions can seem good or even godly on the surface. Without healing and wholeness, a posture of self-sacrifice can actually mask avoidance of dealing with one's own issues, which flows from their own codependency. I cannot stress this enough: ministering from our wounds is detrimental to ourselves and those around us. Ministering from our brokenness, instead of from our breakthrough, will ultimately lead to burnout. This does not demonstrate God's best for us.

Some may ask, how do you know if you are ready to minister to others?

1. First, you have to be gifted in ministering to people. You may be gifted in ministering to others if (a) you have a heart to see others healed emotionally; (b) you have or are in the process of dealing with your own brokenness; (c) your church leadership and others gifted in healing recognize your gifting.

2. If you are a mental health professional, you should practice and spend time observing those skilled in Mind Renewing Healing Prayer. You need to spend much time training and honing your skills like you would in any other modality in which you want to develop proficiency. (Mental health professionals can have a hard time putting aside their training and, metaphorically, stepping out of the

boat of their comfort into the faith-filled waters of dependency on Jesus.)

3. If you are laity, you should submit to the covering of your church and the authority structure of their prayer ministry, if they have one. If not, I do not recommend pursuing ministry on your own. Don't be a lone ranger.

4. If you are greatly triggered when ministering, that means you still need to pursue your own healing before ministering to others.

5. We will all be triggered from time to time, which means we need to make healing a lifestyle, not a one-time event. We need to understand that being triggered is a reminder of our need for continued healing even as we continue to minister.

6. Ultimately we are all "wounded healers," but we must be healthy enough to impart healing to others.

7. Finally, you are compassionate but not codependent and caretaking; you have healthy boundaries.

We need to continue to work on ourselves throughout life as we are emotionally triggered. I highly appreciate and respect those in ministry and ministries who make a yearly provision for their staff members to do their own healing work. This is a personnel investment that yields extremely high returns: it helps the minister, as well as his/her ministry team, to serve more effectively. Unfortunately, it is rarely done.

> *"... let us strip off and throw aside every encumbrance (unnecessary weight) and that sin which so readily (deftly and cleverly) clings to and entangles us, and let us run with patient endurance and steady and active persistence the appointed course of the race that is set before us."*
>
> (HEBREWS 12:1-3, AMPC)

Paul calls us to throw aside our encumbrances and run the race with endurance. What are those encumbrances and unnecessary weights that we carry? I believe they include our emotional triggers. Throughout the years, I have worked with many graduate counseling students who have sat in on my sessions for their required clinical observation. Many times, when a patient is in the midst of processing a painful memory, particularly if they are detailing a terrible abuse, I watch the students' faces and I see their triggered reactions as they observe me minister Mind Renewing Healing Prayer. Later, they will often admit that hearing someone else's account has triggered their own unresolved past issues or abuse, and they have a very difficult time watching the session. They will be unable to effectively lead others to healing until they have completed their own healing journey.

Obviously the same is true or even more so for those who are lay ministers of Mind Renewing Healing Prayer. If we are to experience breakthrough and finish the race of life well, we must deal with our wounded past. We begin with the starting point of the healing process: *emotional triggers.*

CHAPTER 6

EMOTIONAL TRIGGERS,
THE PATHWAY TO HEALING

"David inquired of the Lord, saying, Shall I go up against the Philis-tines? Will You deliver them into my hand? And the Lord said to David, 'Go up, for I will surely deliver [them] into your hand.' And David came to Baal-perazim, and he smote them there, and said, 'The Lord has broken through my enemies before me, like the bursting out of great waters.' So he called the name of that place Baal-perazim [Lord of breaking through]."
(2 SAMUEL 5:19-20, AMPC)

HEALING PRINCIPLE: We must pay attention to our emotional triggers, realizing that they indicate areas of life where we need to pursue healing. Until we locate root memories and experience a revelation of His truth and healing in them, we will continue to be triggered, re-en-acting our lie-based beliefs and unresolved conflicts in daily life. Emotional triggers are the pathway to healing.

The key to a successful life is hearing from the Lord for divine direction and acting on it. The key to healing is choosing to allow God to communicate to us in our triggered state and hearing, receiving and acting upon His truth as David did. God gave David, time and time again, the pathway to victory and overcoming in the midst of severe trial and adversity.

On the day that David encountered the Philistines, he faced a serious life or death crisis as the Philistines came to destroy him after being anointed king. Despite David's state of *woundedness* from many trials and tribulations, he had learned to exercise his *willingness* before the Lord. David made a choice to press in and inquire of the Lord. He chose to listen to and trust in the word and promises that God spoke to him and act upon them. The result of his willingness to depend on God was a tangible, powerful, dramatic breakthrough. Miraculously, the God of the angel armies broke through and totally defeated the enemies of Israel. The Lord revealed Himself to David and now today to us as *Baal-perazim*, the Lord of "breaking through."

David was an extraordinary man. His *wiring* was such that while being an emotional, passionate, creative musician type, he was also a fearless warrior. His *woundedness* may have come from a sense of being invalidated by his family. As the youngest son, he was not considered significant enough even to be called by his father when Samuel came to anoint one of Jesse's sons to be king (see 1 Samuel 16:1-13). Later, when he offered to fight Goliath, he was accused of feeling too highly about himself by his older brothers and was reprimanded to stay in his place as a shepherd (see 1 Samuel 17:26-29). Additionally, David is continuously portrayed throughout Scripture as extremely emotional, struggling with deeply triggered emotions and, at times, depression. We see David struggling with these emotions in 2 Samuel 6, when he responds to a situation out of anger and fear.

"And David became angry because of the Lord's outbreak against Uzzah; and he called the name of the place Perez

Uzzah to this day. David was afraid of the Lord that day; and he said, 'How can the ark of the Lord come to me?'"

(2 SAMUEL 6:8-9, NKJV)

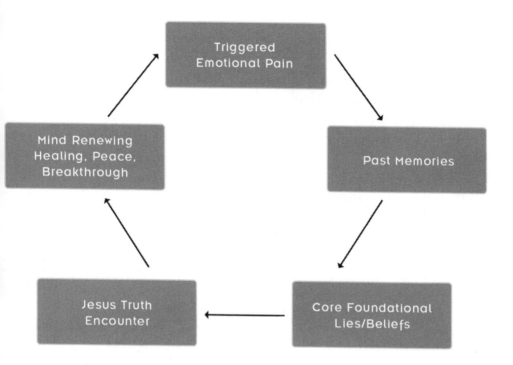

I believe this is an example of David operating out of his triggered emotions. A *triggered emotion* is an emotional *overreaction* to a current life event, situation or circumstance. The life situations that trigger a person to emotionally overreact in their day-to-day life are evidence that they have lie-based thinking. If we follow the trail of our triggered emotional reactions during a Mind Renewing Healing Prayer session we can help the individual find the past memories where their lie-based beliefs are rooted.

THE GOOD, BAD AND UGLY

As painful as it might be, an emotional trigger is an opportunity for breakthrough! When you are emotionally stirred or triggered, the experiential room (the subconscious part of the mind where past memory events reside) is trying to tell you something. This is the place from which we react and where triggered emotional reactions emerge into our current life situations. Whether it be anxiety, panic, guilt or another emotion, you must choose to pay attention to what your triggered emotion is trying to communicate.

Because our emotional triggers are the key to breakthrough, I start Mind Renewing Healing Prayer sessions by tapping into the emotional triggers of the prayer recipient. The good news is that triggered emotional pain is the pathway to healing. The bad news is that emotional triggers cause us pain. They make us feel bad and so we try to medicate or avoid them. It is true that none of us likes to feel painful emotions, myself included, but it is important to remember that our emotional triggers are indicators of where we have been internally wounded and broken. They can lead us to the memories that contain our core lie-based thinking. In this way, triggered emotions are the starting point in a five-stage healing model.

The above formula is a brief overview of the healing prayer process I have used to set thousands of people free on a weekly basis since 1999. I will elaborate on this healing model in later chapters, but for now it is important to note that my goal is to help people prayerfully choose to follow the trail of their triggered emotional reactions to their memories and to invite Jesus into that place. Accessing and following your triggered responses is the beginning of your healing prayer journey.

PERSONAL EXPERIENCE

Triggers can surface for anyone, so I try to practice these healing principles myself. In the summer of 2014, I was at my mother's home in Columbus, Ohio, for my nephew's high school graduation. During my visit, my mom, who had been a healthy 81-year-old woman, had a stroke four hours before my family and I were scheduled to catch a flight back to Virginia. Miraculously, we got her to one of the top ten stroke centers in the United States within 45 minutes. It was a great success, even though it was a stressful, triggering and trying week for everyone. Unbelievably, she was back to walking three miles a day within six weeks.

As thankful as I was for God's goodness that week, I was triggered by the experience. My sister had found my mother in the bathroom when her stroke began, and I had carried her to her bed as we called the paramedics, wondering then and throughout the following week how, or if, she would recover. I returned to my home in Virginia a week after my mom was released from the hospital and returned to my normal routine. When I resumed my pattern of swimming daily laps for 30 minutes in my swimming pool, I started to have fearful thoughts and anxious feelings when I was in the deep end of the pool. I started wondering, *What if I have a stroke in the deep water when no one is home and I drown?* I never had these thoughts before during my daily swimming routine. I was being royally triggered! I *knew* the thoughts were irrational and kept on swimming, but I continued to have them for two or three days. They slowly diminished, but the residue of these triggered emotions and thoughts remained.

At the time, I did what I teach those I minister healing prayer to do: I bookmarked my triggered reaction. Just as you do when you are reading a book, I put a mental bookmark in my mind to remember where I left off in my healing journey. I knew in a few weeks I would be joining my close friend of over 30 years, John Syes, in Wintergreen, Virginia, for a retreat. John is a pastor, counselor and healing prayer minister. We had already planned to fellowship, pray and minister healing prayer to one another, which we do annually, so I bookmarked my triggered reaction until I could get together with John and receive my own Mind Renewing Healing Prayer ministry. A few weeks later when John prayed with me, I focused on my triggered fear and anxiety that surfaced when swimming. I immediately went back to a series of early childhood memories where I had been sick, on and off, for about two years between two and four years of age. During that time I had to go to the doctor for shots two times a week. In those early memories, fear-based beliefs were formed that were activated as an older child whenever I had to go to the doctor for a shot or medical treatment. The fear subsided as I grew older, but those early beliefs were connected to the emotional triggers activated by my mom's stroke. In my early childhood memories, I had developed some *core foundational beliefs* related to fear of illness and pain in medical treatment. Despite my ability to rationalize, I couldn't help but think something bad was going to happen.

> **Core Foundational Belief definition**: a thought typically rooted in early childhood memories that caused you to form a belief that endured into adulthood. These beliefs manifest throughout our life, especially whenever one is emotionally triggered.

> **Example**: If one was raised by a verbally abusive parent, one would typically form a core foundational belief connected to fear ("something bad is going to happen"), as well as feelings of powerlessness ("there's nothing I can do about it"). These feelings would follow them throughout their life whenever situations arise when they are triggered with feelings of fear and helplessness.

I never would have imagined that the emotional reactions that surfaced while I was swimming were actually rooted in those specific early childhood memories, but after processing and receiving the  Lord's truth, it made total sense. This happens for most people to whom I minister. Our defenses can be extremely effective in preventing us from looking at the core memory places where the lie-based thinking is rooted.

As we prayed through the memories where my fear was rooted in my early childhood illness and doctors' visits, the Lord spoke to me through the scripture below that I had always known (in the logical part of my mind), but I had not yet experienced in those early memories. The Lord simply spoke to me, "These light and momentary afflictions are nothing in comparison to the Glory that is to come" (2 Corinthians 4:17). The Lord usually doesn't speak to us with scripture in the Mind Renewing Healing Prayer process, but this time He did and illuminated this to me in a powerful way in my memory as a little boy. In an instant, Jesus, through the Holy Spirit, communicated His truth to me with a simple phrase. As I willed to receive the Lord's truth, my memories instantly received the revelation. In the place of internalized lies and fear from childhood, God's Word took root, resulting in peace, calm and resolution.

What I want to communicate is that the triggering life event you experience, whether it be a stroke or something else, is not the root problem; *lie-based thinking is the root issue.* And until you follow the trigger to the memory where the lies originated and experience a revelation of His truth in them, you will continue to reenact your lie-based beliefs whenever similar life events occur. Luckily, Jesus is more interested in helping us lay hold of the healing He provided for us on the cross than we are to receive it!

THE WAY WE'RE WIRED

When I minister healing prayer to someone at the Meadows Healing Prayer Center, there are times when I am meeting the individual for the first time. I may have some idea of why they are seeking healing, but prior to our first session, I never know for sure what they will present or in what direction the session will go. We always meet in a comfortable and relaxed setting, and I spend the first hour of our first session conducting an assessment and evaluation. Preparation is key and I make sure to provide reading material prior to our appointment that outlines the Mind Renewing Healing Prayer process in detail. I reiterate this process when we meet in person, mindful that the person must always be free to choose the direction they need to take in their healing journey. As I begin to work with a new client, and throughout the time I minister to them on their healing journey, I consider three aspects of their identity: *wiring, woundedness* and *willingness.*

WIRING

We all have been created by God with a unique psychological make-up, strengths and weaknesses. Some of us are introverts or extroverts. Some are very in touch with their emotions; others may be less so. We have our natural gifts, aptitudes and personality traits. *Our wiring is our God-given personality.*

We are all wired differently. Part of respecting someone's *wiring* is remaining open and flexible during ministry to them. For example, I try to tap into a person's wiring and allow their personality traits to express themselves. I try to join them and work at their pace while at the same time keeping them on track to accomplish the healing task at hand. Some people need more prompting or help getting in touch with their emotions. For example, if someone is more cognitive in their wiring, they may not be as in touch with their emotions. I may have to ask them more questions about their feelings in order to help them tap into them. If they have ADHD they may have more difficulties focusing. I will have to spend more time anchoring them in a memory in order to keep them focused in the memory and on what we are doing as their mind will have more of a tendency to roam. (More on *anchoring* in chapters 8-9.)

WOUNDEDNESS

While we are born with our wiring, personality traits, natural attributes, gifts and aptitudes, we are not created with *wounds*. By wounds I mean the places in life, usually in childhood, where we have been wounded, rejected, abused and hurt. Unfortunately, our wounds can alter our God-given personality and how we respond to life. There are a number of ways *woundedness* (the state of being wounded) can present in someone's personality.

> **Emotionally shut down:** Some people are so emotionally shut down and well-defended that I have to help them get in touch with their buried pain and emotions. I ask them questions about what they are feeling and about their

resistance to their emotions.

Intellectualization: Some are overly intellectual; they stay in their head and have difficulty expressing emotions and connecting with their heart. For instance, when I ask them, "What do you feel here in the memory?" They say, "I'm by myself." They can state their *belief,* but cannot express their emotions in a sophisticated way. As I minister to them, I respect their pace as I help them reconnect with their heart. I help them to identify and feel their emotions, which brings them to the ultimate goal of identifying their lie-based beliefs.

Denial: The deeply wounded are experts at diverting, denying and suppressing their feelings. I help them connect with their emotions and their heart. In most cases they have learned to bury and medicate their pain by caretakers who are equally out of touch with their emotions. It is akin to having an atrophied muscle. We need to give those who are deeply wounded or numb permission and encouragement to connect with their heart and face their pain. I want to respect their pace, which also has to do with their wiring. It is important to minister in the power of the Holy Spirit's leading and anointing as I help them exercise their underused emotional muscle again.

Dissociation: Dissociation can occur when children are traumatized and abused sexually and physically. It can also occur when they go through severe emotional and physical pain, medical procedures, accidents and surgeries. Dissociation is a defensive choice, made especially under the age of five or six, and happens outside one's conscious awareness. The mind has the ability to protect the child by dissociating painful memory, emotions and physical pain, totally out of one's conscious awareness. God has put within the brain the ability to protect us by disconnecting from painful memories, emotions, and body memories.

The defense mechanisms listed above are the primary ones. We may operate with other defense mechanisms as well such as projection, compartmentalization, displacement, rationalization and repression, which have to be worked through in the healing process. As a byproduct of one's woundedness, one may display more symptoms, such as depression, anxiety, panic attacks, low self- esteem and anger. One may also be more likely to struggle with addictions to alcohol, substances, food, sex, work, codependency in order to numb their pain from their woundedness.

Despite the personality traits, gifts and attributes with which we were created, our wounding can, and often will, set us back in life. Satan's plan is to diminish us through our past wounds, hurts and mental strongholds, so when ministering to someone you will have to carefully consider their personal history and family dysfunction as you walk with them on their healing journey.

WILLINGNESS

Willingness is crucial in assessing one's openness to be healed. One must be willing to feel, visit one's pain, look at the truth about one's life, and release anger, rage and resentments at the deepest level in order to be free. Willingness is demonstrated not just in word but is shown by a person's actions to do the deep painful healing work that is needed to be free and to live a victorious overcoming life.

Janice's Story

There is a woman named Janice whom I have worked with for some time. Now in her early sixties, she is one of the most severely sexually and physically abused women I have seen in my practice. At times, she has been a challenge for me to work with, especially in our earliest sessions, because her need was so great. What helped me to keep working with Janice was that I saw her tremendous will, to not only survive, but to move forward in her healing journey, as painful as it was. When I first started working with Janice, her mind was highly dissociated and fragmented. Today, she is increasingly in touch with her emotions, body and heart. She now ministers effectively to others in a variety of settings and is an asset and blessing to all she encounters. This is wholly due to her willingness to work through her deeply triggered pain and to allow the Lord to do all that He promises in His Word.

Some people come to me for a Mind Renewing Healing Prayer session with fewer wounds than Janice but are unwilling to delve into the deep places required to find their freedom. On occasion, I have worked with others who experience a breakthrough in a healing prayer session once or twice but who choose not to come back to continue to do the deeper work that is needed. As the old sports metaphor goes, "no pain, no gain." Some are not willing to press into their pain and grief even for a great result or gain. The ability to delay gratification is a huge part of personal growth and healing.

We can help people work through their resistance to their healing during a Mind Renewing Healing Prayer session. We can help them to identify the reasons for their resistance and move forward on their healing journey, but ultimately each person must choose to walk out their healing journey. God will not violate our deepest will, so neither should we when working with prayer recipients. We must respect their freedom of choice to heal.

TRIGGERS IN OUR HOMES AND FAMILIES

A triggered emotional reaction can come in many forms and may happen anywhere, at any time. Recognizing them is important and knowing they can occur even in seemingly insignificant life situations will help you identify them when they surface. If a triggered reaction happens in a seemingly insignificant situation, you can be assured it will happen in a greater way when big, real-life crises occur. The most common situations in which triggers occur are at home with our families, as well as with our families of origin. Most people also are triggered in the workplace and with our church family. However, most of us experience our greatest triggers with those we spend the most time with: spouses, parents and children.

FAMILY TRIGGERS

MARITAL TRIGGERS

I believe that most marriage problems are, at least partially, rooted in unresolved triggered emotional reactions with one another that are then projected onto your mate. That is not to say that your mate does not do some incredibly annoying things that irritate you; you still need to work through common marital issues such as communication, sex, finances, in-laws and a multitude of other issues. *However, I have found that most marital conflicts have to do with each person's own triggered emotional reactions, rooted in their past brokenness.* Luckily, dealing with our marital triggers can greatly improve how one deals with one's marriage.

I have found that if we will own our part of the problem, including our triggered reactions, we can respond better to our mate, regardless of their response to us. This is personally empowering because it helps us understand that there is always something we can do about the situations we face in marriage. Even better, if a husband and wife *both* choose to own their triggered reactions and engage in Mind Renewing Healing Prayer to work on their own issues, a couple can place themselves in a position for optimal relational growth, healing, mind renewal and breakthrough. This can result in a vastly improved, healthier marital relationship.

PARENTING TRIGGERS

It is advantageous for us as parents to respond to our triggers in our parenting. This is a great opportunity for our own healing and for improved parent-child relationships. A parenting trigger is simply when you are emotionally triggered and overreact in your role as parent. We all do it, but some do it to a degree that is detrimental in one's role as a parent and that causes problems for one's children. A parent may be triggered, overreacting and responding in anger, fear or feeling out of control. When we feel out of control I have witnessed some parents regress and respond in a childlike, powerless, out-of-control manner, rendering them unable to adequately discipline and parent their children. Unfortunately, when some parents are triggered, they respond in a harsh, controlling and abusive fashion that is very damaging to the child's psyche.

CHILDHOOD TRIGGERS

Nothing can be more triggering to children than unhealthy interactions with their parents. Most of the reasons adults come into therapy and Mind Renewing Healing Prayer have to do with wounds they received in childhood from wounded, broken parents. That is why it is crucial to deal with your wounds *now*; if you don't, your past unresolved conflicts will resurface in the next generation. If you do not face the truth about your life and allow God's truth to heal you and set you free, it will leak into your parenting relationships and interactions and will infect your children.

The more dysfunctional and wounded a parent or family system is, the less likely they are to be aware of how their parenting actions and words may impact and wound their children. Dysfunctional, wounded parents do not take responsibility for their actions; they act blameless in the face of fault and yet shame their children. Healthy parents have the ability to take responsibility for their triggered reactions and responses, admit when they are wrong and say "I'm sorry" to their children and move forward. Being a healthy person and parent requires living in, reacting to and responding from the place of truth.

WORK AND MINISTRY TRIGGERS

When we spend eight or more hours a day at work, we will invariably, as at home, find people and situations that trigger us. The annoying co-worker, the controlling boss, as well as a variety of other situations, provide the fodder to be triggered at work. These situations provide opportunities for our continued healing. The same principle applies to people in any aspect of ministry. Pastors get triggered with parishioners and vice versa. It is a common place of reenactment of our unresolved family of origin, especially father, issues. I'm afraid too many pastors have felt "called to another place," when conflict arises in the church. In reality, if they had pursued their own healing in regard to their triggered reactions, they might have been able to work through the conflict, grow and see "all things work together for good." If you're on the mission field, you may come into triggered conflict with those whom you work and vice versa. They will also invariably encounter the extreme triggers of adapting to another culture coupled with triggered reactions of loneliness and isolation. There are countless ways this happens, but, once again, they are all opportunities for each person to own their triggered reactions and pursue healing.

FEAR, ANXIETY AND PANIC TRIGGERS

Kimberly's Story

In the same way that interpersonal relationships can trigger us, emotional triggers may also occur in close proximity to certain stimuli. For example, I worked with a woman named Kimberly who had an extreme fear of bridges and heights but had to travel cross-country for her session with me. On the way to her visit, she had to drive across several massive bridges. She was so emotionally triggered, she had to stop the car to collect herself each time she approached a bridge. When we began to pray during her first session, I had her close her eyes, feel and focus on the triggered emotional and physical reactions she experienced when she encountered bridges and heights. I had her focus in on her fear, panic, anxiety, heart palpitations and shortness of breath. A memory emerged when she was seven years old. In the memory, she approached a bridge while walking and saw a man standing on a bridge that brought up these same emotions. As she focused on her fear and panic, she went to a memory she had not remembered in over 35 years. She remembered this man molesting her and a friend the day before at the side of a store in her neighborhood. She had not remembered the part of the memory where the molestation occurred in many years; however, every time she came to a bridge she experienced this triggered reaction. Her mind, through her triggers, was trying to communicate something to her that she was not ready to deal with until that day in my office. As I helped her process through the memory as the seven-year-old, she identified her lie-based thinking. In addition to feeling fear, panic and anxiety, she felt powerless, dirty, ashamed and angry. These are the same triggered emotions she experienced each time she approached bridges or heights.

As we walked through the memory together, Jesus communicated His truth to her. She received His truth totally, and peace, calm and resolution flooded the memory. It was an amazing thing to witness as His truth integrated into her present, conscious awareness. On a follow-up call four months later, she reported no more fear of bridges and heights. After 35 years of suffering and incapacitation due to panic and fear, she was now free—praise the Lord! Only Jesus can do this!

IT'S ALL ABOUT YOU!

How many of you need a breakthrough? I encourage you to ask for and expect God to intervene in your brokenness, right in the midst of your triggered reactions. Remember, even if others trigger us, our pathway to healing is owning our triggered reactions and moving into our own healing despite others. It's all about you, regardless of what others may do. Allow Him to break through into your triggered, wounded state whenever and wherever it occurs. I have the privilege of seeing God regularly bring healing to those who choose to receive. I have seen thousands of people receive healing and breakthrough and, because of this, I know that it is possible for you and those to whom you minister.

Like David, most of us will experience our greatest triggered reactions in the midst of crisis and conflict. And like David, the Lord desires to reveal Himself as *Baal-perazim, the Lord of breaking through,* to you and your circumstances. I firmly believe that the God of angel armies is literally battling on our behalf, ministering to and helping us to overcome in life, especially in our healing journeys. His kingdom is more real than our earthly realm, which will pass away. Our bodies, our hurts and wounds, our various problems will someday pass away. The beauty is, in the midst of this world, He said to pray daily, "Thy kingdom come, thy will be done, on earth as it is in heaven." We get to pray for and experience His kingdom now! We must press in to Jesus and allow His kingdom to come and His will to be done, in, around and through us, on Earth as it is in heaven.

CHAPTER 7

TYPES OF LIE-BASED THINKING

---

*"What you're after is truth from the inside out. Enter me, then; con-
ceive a new, true life."*
(PSALM 51:6, MSG)

HEALING PRINCIPLE: During a Mind Renewing Healing Prayer session, I often ask questions to help a person identify their sense of
worth and value in their core beliefs in past memories. Finding God's
truth, especially in our worth and value, core beliefs, is central to finding freedom in Christ and walking in our true identity.

As we discussed in the previous chapter, triggered emotions are not entirely negative. Ultimately, triggers lead us to discover the lies we believe. When we are in relationship with Jesus, who is the Way, the Truth and the Life, we know how to uproot these lies and walk into our healing. In my experience, I have learned that most lies fall into eight categories.[1]

If you would like to identify your lie-based beliefs after reviewing each of the eight categories, you can do so by determining which of the phrases associated with each lie feel true to you. Then, lift up the lie-based beliefs, one by one, unto the Lord. Finally, ask Jesus what He wants you to know. Here are a few tips to help you in this healing exercise.

- Close your eyes.
- Focus on and embrace the lie-based belief and feel the emotion around it.
- Ask Jesus what He wants you to know about your lie-based beliefs.
- *Listen.* Don't just focus on the correct biblical answer from the analytical part of your mind, but pay attention to what you actually see, sense or hear Jesus communicate to you about your belief.
- Does what He communicates feel true to you? For example, *"It's not your fault." "I am here for you!"*
- Remember, you should always judge what you sense the Lord communicating to you by the Bible, His written Word.

1. FEAR-BASED LIES

Fear-based lies come from scary life experiences. They may arise if a person was terrorized or if their life was threatened in childhood.

---

[1]These types and categories are taken indirectly from Dr. Ed Smith, the founder of Theophostic Ministry. See *Theophostic Prayer Ministry, Basic Training Seminar Manual,* pp. 47-62.

(Obviously, fear can arise in adulthood as well, but most core memories are rooted in childhood.) Fear-based beliefs can also originate from exposure to scary images or scenes, which may happen if you watched scary movies or TV shows at an early age. One of my fear-based memories is linked to an episode of *The Twilight Zone*, a TV show that I used to watch as a child. That was not a particularly frightening show, but I recently was surprised as I discovered one of my fear-based beliefs was rooted in an episode. Images and film have a profound impact on children and have the potential to produce effects that last throughout adulthood.

It's important to recognize if fear is governing your life so you know how to be free from it. Some phrases that I often hear in session that alert me to a fear-based mindset include:

Something bad is going to happen.

I am going to die.

They are hurting me.

If I tell, he will hurt me.

If I trust, I will get hurt.

It is just a matter of time before it happens again.

They are going to get me.

He is coming back to do it again.

I cannot make a decision or something will go wrong.

Do any of these phrases feel true to you? Remember, it's not whether or not they *are* true that matters; it's whether or not they *feel* true. Emotional triggers mean that we live and react from what feels true to us, thereby revealing our true belief system in the experiential part of our mind. Fear is common, but it doesn't have to be. If we want to walk in victory, we need to lay these ungodly beliefs to rest at the foot of the cross. The Bible says, "There is no fear in love; but perfect love casts out fear, because fear involves torment. But he who fears has not been made perfect in love" (1 John 4:18,

NKJV). Indeed, it is reasonable to assume that any fear, anxiety and panic-based emotions, especially irrational ones, are unnecessary. We experience fear and other triggered emotions because of core, lie-based beliefs. The good news is that we can be free from them as we pursue our healing journey.

2. ABANDONMENT-BASED LIES

These lies are rooted in past memories where people have experienced rejection and abandonment. For example, an abandonment-based lie may take root in a child's psyche if divorce, illness, addiction or mental instability prevented one or both parents from being emotionally or physically present with the child. They may have been latchkey children who were left at home alone frequently. Adopted children in particular often fall into this category, as they typically carry a very deep sense of rejection and harbor wounds from abandonment. But not all abandonment-based lies are a result of parent-based relationships. Some children may come from healthy loving homes but may have experienced rejection or bullying from peers. Examples of abandonment-based lies include:

I am abandoned.

I am not needed.

I am all alone.

I will always be alone.

There is no one to protect me.

God has forsaken me.

No one will believe me.

I can't trust anyone.

I have been betrayed by everyone.

As I've stated at length, we can "know the truth," yet not be free. When people have core abandonment lies, they often feel abandoned and unloved by God as well. I often hear phrases like, "Where was He? Why did He allow me to be born to people who didn't want me, treat me right and were not there for me?" People who feel abandoned are often emotionally well-defended and can give off strong defensive vibrations to others, much like a porcupine defending with its quills. They tend toward the extremes: they may push people away or become very needy. Those who have abandonment-based lies often experience shame-based lies as well. The Bible says, "Be strong and of good courage, do not fear nor be afraid of them; for the Lord your God, He is the One who goes with you. He will not leave you nor forsake you….And the Lord, He is the One who goes before you. He will be with you, He will not leave you nor forsake you; do not fear nor be dismayed" (Deuteronomy 31:6,8, NKJV).

3. SHAME AND GUILT-BASED LIES

I grew up in the Free Methodist Church. My father was a pastor in an evangelical Bible-believing church where the gospel was openly preached and altar calls were regularly given so congregants had the opportunity to receive Christ's salvation. Even as a boy, I remember wondering why some of the same people kept coming forward for the altar call repentance and prayer. I wondered why they kept returning, seemingly to pray the sinner's prayer, and why they had not yet experienced breakthrough in their life. It was as if they kept coming back to *repent for the same thing over and over again.* I was puzzled, but now I realize that many of those people were dealing with shame and guilt-based beliefs, deeply rooted in their past wounds. While I'm sure they had normal problems for which they needed prayer and support from time to time, I am certain that much of their present guilt and shame was triggered by their past shame and guilt lies. This is not what the Lord intends for us.

"…I came that they may have and enjoy life, and have it in abundance [to the full, till it overflows]."

(JOHN 10:10, AMP)

"What then shall we say to these things? If God is for us, who can be against us?...Yet in all these things we are more than conquerors through Him who loved us."

(ROMANS 8:31,37, NKJV)

Below are some typical shame lies. Do any of these feel true to you?

What happened was my fault.

I caused him/her to act that way.

I felt pleasure, so I wanted it.

I am stupid, ignorant, an idiot for not_____.

I should have done something to stop it from happening.

If I had been a better child, my parents would have never broken up.

Had I been there, he would not have died.

I deserved it.

I was a participant.

I should have known better.

I should have told someone.

I knew what was going to happen, yet I stayed anyway.

It happened because of my looks...my gender...my body.

I did not try to run away.

I can never be forgiven for having that abortion.

I am cheap.

I kept going back.

4. TAINTED LIES

Tainted lies are similar to the shame lies. Both are related to one's state of being but differ based on the person responsible for the negative action related to one's state of being. For example, guilt says, "I did something bad." Shame says, "I am bad." A tainted lie suggests that I am bad, not because of what I have done, but because of what was done to me. These lies are common in people who have experienced sexual abuse or trauma. The abuse or rape victim may feel they are marked, hurt, damaged, dirty or perverted because of the acts committed against them. They feel they will always be broken because of what happened to them. Literally or metaphorically, they may feel connected to their abuser and have a sense that they will never fully detach their bodies from the forced physical connection that occurred. The tainted category of lies shows up in statements such as:

> *I am dirty/shameful/evil/perverted because of what happened to me.*
>
> *My life is ruined.*
>
> *I will never feel clean again.*
>
> *Everyone can see my shame...filth...dirtiness.*
>
> *I will always be hurt/damaged/broken because of what happened.*
>
> *I will never be happy because this happened.*
>
> *My body is dirty.*
>
> *What he did marked me for life.*
>
> *I can never be the same after what happened.*

The Bible says,

> *"You are already clean because of the word which I have spoken to you."*
>
> (JOHN 15:3, NKJV)

> *"Let us all come forward and draw near with true (honest and sincere) hearts in unqualified assurance and absolute*

conviction engendered by faith (by that leaning of the entire human personality on God in absolute trust and confidence in His power, wisdom, and goodness), having our hearts sprinkled and purified from a guilty (evil) conscience and our bodies cleansed with pure water."

(HEBREWS 11:22-23, AMPC)

How awesome that our great God cleanses our inner man, our hearts, from a guilty conscience. He also washes our outer man, our bodies, from the sexual and other defiling things we have done, as well as the things done to us where we were victimized, with *His pure cleansing water.*

5. HOPELESSNESS LIES

This type of lie comes from believing that there is *no way out, no options, no way of escape* and *the situation is not going to get better.* They have feelings of hopelessness, depression and despair. They feel that there is no light at the end of the tunnel. This type of lie leads to depressive, despairing and hopeless emotions. Lies of hopelessness breed the following types of statements and beliefs:

My only escape is to die.

It is never going to get any better.

There is no way out.

There is no good thing for me.

I have no reason to live.

The only option I have is death.

There are no options available to me.

There is nothing that I can do.

I used to work in a fifth floor office that had a beautiful view; I could see several miles away into downtown Norfolk. The windows were tinted, but you wouldn't have known it to look at them: on a sunny day, it still looked sunny outside the window. However, when you went outside it was much brighter. On a cloudy overcast day, it looked really dreary, dark and foreboding. In fact, when a depressed person would come into my office they would sometimes comment on how dreary it was outside. I would remind them that these were tinted windows and that it was not as dreary and dark as it looked outside these windows. I would use that opportunity to share that as a metaphor for their depression. I would remind them that feeling depressed and hopeless is like wearing tinted glasses; in a depressed state, people view the world through lenses that make situations appear darker and drearier.[2]

The Bible says,

> *"Praise be to the God and Father of our Lord Jesus Christ! In his great mercy he has given us new birth into a living hope through the resurrection of Jesus Christ from the dead, and into an inheritance that can never perish, spoil or fade. This inheritance is kept in heaven for you, who through faith are shielded by God's power until the coming of the salvation that is ready to be revealed in the last time. In all this you greatly rejoice, though now for a little while you may have had to suffer grief in all kinds of trials."*
>
> (1 PETER 1:3-6, NIV)

6. POWERLESS LIES

Powerless lies are similar to the hopelessness lies. The difference

---

[2]There are certainly situations where people are experiencing a legitimate clinical depression where antidepressant medications are indicated. The depressed may feel like there is no way out, and this can lead to suicidal ideation. That is the power of a lie that is entrenched deeply in one's psyche. Those who are depressed and suicidal will need a licensed mental health professional and a psychiatric consult for a possible medication evaluation. If you are a pastoral counselor or lay healing prayer minister, I would recommend you work alongside a Christian mental health professional in these cases. If no Christian professional is available, they still may need professional evaluation and assessment.

between the two is that those who feel powerless may see a way out of their situation, but they feel powerless to make it happen. (Those who feel hopeless do not believe they have any options and that there is no way out.) Those who suffer with powerless lies have usually been controlled and abused. The core lie was formed in childhood in a place where they were or felt controlled, powerless and restrained. Now, when triggered by a similar situation, the feeling of powerlessness is triggered. For instance, when a childhood abuse victim comes across an overpowering, controlling personality as an adult, they may freeze in a childlike state of anxiety or intimidation. They are being triggered as their core lie-based beliefs are being activated. This could be triggered in an interaction with an authority figure, such as their boss, pastor, or marriage partner. They may feel tongue-tied, intimidated, fearful or voiceless.

Years ago, I had a female client who had a very controlling, abusive husband. I asked her why she did not call the police and have him arrested after he had beaten her up. She said that he always told her that he knew the police in their area and, laughingly, told her they would do nothing if she called them. Because of her past abuse and core lies of powerlessness, she believed him and never questioned him. Abusers seek victimized people who feel powerless; they prey on them and may even marry them. A few months later, this woman's husband almost beat her to death. Her nine-year-old son witnessed this horrible event and ran to the neighbors to call the police. To her complete shock and surprise, the police came, handcuffed and arrested her husband. They took him to jail and a restraining order was granted.

Unfortunately, as this happened, she also learned that her husband had physically abused and sexually molested their children as well. After she learned this devastating news, I worked on empowering her to break through her deeply entrenched powerlessness lie-based beliefs. In response, she learned to set boundaries that would keep her and her children safe for the first time in her life. She ultimately divorced her unrepentant husband, who never took responsibility for his actions. In cases like this, we see the importance of breaking through lies of powerlessness: as a childhood abuse victim, the cycles of powerless thinking almost cost this woman her life.

Some examples of some powerless lies include:

I know what needs to be done, but I am powerless to do it.

I need to take care of people, but I can't.

They are too strong for me to resist.

I am overwhelmed.

I am too little to make it stop.

Everything is out of control.

I am pulled from every direction.

I am too small, weak and helpless to do anything.

"I have strength for all things in Christ Who empowers me [I am ready for anything and equal to anything through Him Who infuses inner strength into me; I am self-sufficient in Christ's sufficiency]."

(PHILIPPIANS 4:13, AMPC)

7. INVALIDATION LIES

Invalidation lies are often clustered with abandonment, shame and hopeless lies. In dysfunctional families where children are not honored, valued and blessed, the invalidation lie is easily planted. Parents who themselves were raised by emotionally absent parents have their own invalidation lies and invalidate their own children, many times without being fully aware of it.

In ministering healing prayer to people, I find that when a curse is spoken by a parent or caretaker over someone, the deepest sense of invalidation can take place. Obviously, if a parent communicates "I wish you were never born" to their child, they instill a deep sense of rejection in their child. Even seemingly benign comments such as, "We were so disappointed when you were born because we always wanted a boy," or "Your birth was not planned, you were a surprise," can wreak havoc on innocent, impressionable children. Of course, invalidation lies can be communicated in many ways.

Years ago, I had a client who had been the star athlete of his football and basketball teams in high school. His alcoholic father never once attended any of his games or ever shared an affirming word for his son. During every game, he was usually the high scorer in basketball and, accordingly, a hero to the school and town. During every game, he always looked up to the bleachers to see if his father might finally have come to validate him. But his dad never came. Never feeling loved or affirmed by his dad, his success was bittersweet. At the age of 35 years, he ended up in my office; accused of molesting a young child, his life was in shambles.

Spoken or implied, curses are the ultimate invalidation lies. As a deep sense of rejection bleeds into every aspect of the person's life, the person's identity becomes deeply damaged. Some phrases I hear associated with invalidation lies include:

I am unlovable.

I am not needed.

I am worthless.

I don't matter.

I was a mistake, and I should have never been born.

I am in the way.

Girls are less important than boys.

Boys are less important that girls.

God could never love or accept me.

I am defective.

There is something wrong with me.

The Bible says,

> "For in Him the whole fullness of Deity (the Godhead) continues to dwell in bodily form [giving complete expression of the divine nature]. And you are in Him, made full and having come to fullness of life [in Christ you too are filled with the Godhead—Father, Son and Holy Spirit—and reach full spiritual stature]. And He is the Head of all rule and authority [of every angelic principality and power]."
>
> (COLOSSIANS 2:9-10 AMPC)

8. CONFUSION LIES

This type of lie is typical in young children, even those who are preverbal or who are at an early age and do not understand what is happening to them. On occasion these lies can be innocently imparted as confusion by misinterpretation. I have a good friend who is a pastor. He told a true story about taking his young, one-year-old son to the doctor for a shot. His one-year-old son was squirming and the doctor asked the father to hold the child still on his lap while the doctor gave him a shot. The father, a very kind and gentle soul, held him still while the doctor gave his squirming son the shot. His son looked up at his dad with a very frightened, confused and distressed look. My friend says he will never forget the look his son gave him. It was as if to communicate to his father, who had been nothing but kind, nurturing and loving with his son, "Why would you allow this man [the doctor] to hurt me and cause me such pain?" The father was saddened and distressed as his son looked at him in such pain and confusion. It also gave the father a deeper revelation of the heavenly Father, who, at times, allows us to go through difficulties that we do not understand. However innocent, it was still easy for the young son to be confused by what was happening in this situation.

Unfortunately, the vast majority of the time, children feel confused when bad things occur to them that they do not understand.

Why would a father, who is supposed to take care of and protect the family, hurt or beat their mother? Why would a parent hurt and abuse them? When early childhood sexual or physical abuse occurs, especially in preverbal children, there is a profound sense of confusion: *Why would they do this to me? Why would an adult relative or a stranger touch me in this private place?* Sometimes, the internal conflict is so great that a traumatic childhood event is dissociated out of their conscious awareness. The triggered responses remain intact however. In other words, a confused feeling state emerges in their adult life when a similar event triggers them. Then, they may respond with a preverbal or very young, seemingly irrational reaction.

Finally, confusion can also be a symptom of *demonization.* It is possible for demonization to occur when someone reacts with a confused emotional response during a Mind Renewing Healing Prayer session. Demons love it when young children are victimized and the confusion lie is planted in their psyche. They don't fight fair. The demon can stir up confusion as a way to prevent someone from looking at their memory content, feeling the pain and identifying the lies. *Demons cannot violate our deepest will, and they cannot reside in the mind without the individual being complicit on some level.* If, however, the ministry recipient is denying or avoiding memory content, they may give an opening for a demonic entity to give them a solution. They authorize the demon to have authority over a part of their mind, however small, which strengthens the confusion further.

The confusion lie is primarily lie-based, but at times could indicate demonic interference. That is more likely to happen with a dissociated, traumatized person. Ultimately, God is not the author of confusion and He desires to bring us to a place of resolution, truth and clarity.

> *"For God is not the author of confusion but of peace, as in all the churches of the saints."*
>
> (1 CORINTHIAN 14:33, NKJV)

In closing, recognizing our core lie-based beliefs is essential to finding healing and breakthrough. As we target our core lie-based beliefs with the weapons of warfare, Jesus, the living Word, we are well on our way to mind-renewal breakthrough and overcoming!

CHAPTER 8

PREREQUISITES AND PREPARATION
FOR MIND RENEWING HEALING PRAYER

---

*"and be renewed in the spirit of your mind, and that you put on
the new man which was created according to God, in true
righteousness and holiness."*
(Ephesians 4:23-24 NKJV)

HEALING PRINCIPLE: Preparing a healing prayer recipient for a
Mind Renewing Healing Prayer session is similar to preparing great
foundation on which to build a house. The more thoroughly you
prepare the prayer recipient to receive ministry, like the house
foundation, the more likely they will experience mind-renewal,
healing and breakthrough!

In the following chapters in this section, we will shift our attention to preparing someone for a Mind Renewing Healing Prayer session. Until this point, everything I have written about builds a foundation for the Mind Renewing Healing Prayer process. From here on, I will explain how to put the foundational principles into practice.

Let me begin by saying, this book is not meant to fully train you to facilitate Mind Renewing Healing Prayer ministry to others. Instead, my goal is to share my perspective on the healing principles for those who are already healing-prayer ministers and therapists, as well as for those who want to grow in their understanding and receive direction and insight into their own healing journey. My goal is to prepare you to open your hearts and minds to embark upon your own healing journey. In the future I hope to write material geared towards training the healing-prayer minister in the Mind Renewing Healing Prayer principles.

PRE-SESSION PREPARATION

A sample preparation package may look something like this:

- Reading Material
- Evaluation/Assessment
- Helpful Diagrams
- The Role of Free Will and Choice
- Anchoring
- Jesus Revealing Truth
- Follow-Up

READING MATERIAL

Prior to accepting a new client for a session, I always send reading material in advance of our first session that explains the Mind Renewing Healing Prayer process. That helps them review and more deeply understand the healing process before we begin, and ensures that the recipient is fully committed to the process before arrival. I send them articles I have written on healing prayer and recommend reading this book in preparation, all of which can be found at MeadowsHealingPrayerCenter.com.

EVALUATION AND ASSESSMENT

The first time I meet with a client or prayer recipient, I spend the first hour of the first session evaluating and assessing their life circumstances, triggered emotional reactions, symptoms, history of psychological problems, addictions and dysfunctional generational family patterns. I assess their sexual history, as well as their history of abuse and trauma. Finally, I look at their spiritual journey and heritage from their family system, including involvement in Christian cults, non-biblical religious experiences, and involvement in any of the following: occult, New Age, Freemasonry and non-Christian religious experiences. The goal of evaluating and assessing is to see what are the issues, symptoms and emotional triggers for which they are seeking help, to determine if they are appropriate candidates to receive Mind Renewing Healing Prayer, and to prepare them for the process.

At that first meeting, before doing anything, I detail how the healing-prayer process works for the recipient so they know exactly what to expect for the remainder of our session. Just as I have done in this book, I have learned that it is important to lay a foundation upon which both the prayer minister and the recipient can share reasonable expectations. Because I am accustomed to holding sessions that last anywhere from 45-minutes to multiple 8-hour days, I tailor the explanation time so that it is appropriate for each recipient.[1]

---

[1] If I am seeing a client for a 45-minute counseling session, I reserve our first session for assessment and evaluation and save Mind Renewing Healing Prayer for the next session. In this case, I don't talk about the Mind Renewing Healing Prayer process for more than 10 or 15 minutes.

HELPFUL DIAGRAMS

Images are powerful teaching tools, so I often use them to explain concepts that are foundational to Mind Renewing Healing Prayer. For example, I draw a diagram of two boxes to illustrate the logical and experiential rooms, which we discussed earlier in this book. I do this to explain the concept of bridging the logical and experiential parts of our mind and also to bring up the topic of defense mechanisms. I explain that it may be difficult for them to feel, release anger, visit a memory or move past an inner wall of resistance. Using the imagery of a door, I explain that inner healing sometimes brings a unique inner struggle. With one hand, you may try to open a door into one part of your mind to access a painful memory, but with your other hand, you may be holding the door shut with even greater force. Try as you might, the door will remain shut until your deeper, inner self is in full agreement to open the door to healing. Usually this inner resistance arises from a desire to self-protect, but actually the results prove that the opposite is true. Resistance to dealing with our pain, which at one time helped us survive, actually becomes a hindrance to our healing and thriving.

The prayer recipient is usually consciously unaware of what's causing their resistance. We are often unaware of the part of self that holds the door shut, that prevents us from moving forward. Explaining these concepts in advance usually helps them move through their resistance more effectively when we begin a Mind Renewing Healing Prayer session.

THE ROLE OF FREE WILL AND CHOICE

I will address *free will and choice* at length later in this book, but it is always a topic I address with my clients before we begin a session. Neither God nor I will violate a person's will in their healing journey. Instead, they must be fully engaged and make repeated choices to move deeper into healing. They must choose to feel, visit the memories that emerge, release their anger and emotions to the Lord, and to forgive. Engaging the will is a powerful exercise, and it ultimately opens the door to great possibilities for healing, restoration and breakthrough.

ANCHORING

Anchoring is a simple, but critical, component to Mind Renewing Healing Prayer. Anchoring, as it relates to healing-prayer, means that the prayer recipient must stay connected to or anchored in their feelings as they process through their memories. Most root memories form in childhood and I want the individual to feel the emotions they experienced in the memories they process through. Doing this helps open the door to the experiential part of the mind by allowing them to connect with their current triggers, leading them to what feels *true* in past, root memories.

JESUS REVEALING TRUTH

Jesus is the Way, the Truth and the Life, and He loves to communicate to us, His beloved children. In Mind Renewing Healing Prayer sessions, I primarily see Him communicating truth in memory. I facilitate this process but allow the prayer recipient to report what they *see, sense* or *hear* Jesus communicating to them. That is not cognitive knowledge; rather, it is a revelation as He communicates to them in memory as they embrace the lies, feel the pain and allow Him to reveal His truth. As He does, the triggered pain gloriously disappears and beautiful breakthrough occurs.

FOLLOW-UP

After the initial intake, for a short, 45-minute diagnostic session, I ask them to share briefly about their week. I do this to assess progress but also so that the prayer recipient can recognize how far they've come in their own healing journey. I usually limit this to about 5 minutes or so. Depending on the day, I may ask any of the following questions:

How are you doing?

Have you experienced any triggering events or situations?

Are you feeling any triggering emotions presently?

What progress have you seen this week?

Are you noticing any situations in which you are less triggered?

Are you feeling any better about yourself?

PART THREE

THE MIND RENEWING HEALING PRAYER PROCESS

CHAPTER 9

THE MIND RENEWING HEALING PRAYER PROCESS

"The Spirit of the Lord God is upon me, because the Lord has anointed and qualified me to preach the Gospel of good tidings to the meek, the poor, and afflicted; He has sent me to bind up and heal the brokenhearted, to proclaim liberty to the [physical and spiritual] captives and the opening of the prison and of the eyes to those who are bound, To proclaim the acceptable year of the Lord [the year of His favor] and the day of vengeance of our God, to comfort all who mourn, To grant [consolation and joy] to those who mourn in Zion— to give them an ornament (a garland or diadem) of beauty instead of ashes, the oil of joy instead of mourning, the garment of praise instead of a heavy, burdened, and failing spirit—that they may be called oaks of righteousness [lofty, strong, and magnificent, distinguished for uprightness, justice, and right standing with God], the planting of the Lord, that He may be glorified."
(ISAIAH 61:1-3, AMPC)

HEALING PRINCIPLE: If your emotional pain and triggered responses persist after prayer, meditation on Scripture and the pursuit of wise counsel, you may be struggling with a chronic life pattern as a reaction to your core lie-based beliefs. It is time to go deeper. You need to allow the Lord to do the healing work that only He can do. If you are experiencing recurring patterns of depression, fear, anxiety, panic attacks, or if you are struggling with continual guilt, shame, unworthiness, condemnation, hopelessness or despair, it is time to encounter Jesus through Mind Renewing Healing Prayer.

I begin a Mind Renewing Healing Prayer session with a recipient by inviting the Holy Spirit to come through opening prayer. While there is no specific *formula* to the process, there are crucial *steps and principles* that enable the prayer minister to effectively minister to the prayer recipient. I typically start a session by asking the prayer recipient to close their eyes while I pray and invoke God's Presence. An opening prayer may look like this:

> *"Holy Spirit, I invite Your Presence and welcome You into this session. I ask that You would help (prayer recipient's name) to feel comfortable and relaxed. I ask for Your anointing and the gifts and power of the Holy Spirit to operate and manifest in this session. I ask for all the resources of Your Kingdom. I ask that You would help (name) to let down their defenses and allow to come up whatever needs to surface now in Jesus' name. I ask You to surround this office with Your protection and care and to help (name) to engage their will at the deepest level. I thank You that, when we pray, You always show up, and that You are available to heal, restore and renew Your children. In Jesus' name, amen!"*

As I open the session in prayer, I ask the recipient to discern and acknowledge (with their eyes closed) any uncomfortable emotions, body sensations or images that surfaced during the opening prayer. I may ask them, "What emotions are you feeling as I pray?" Then, I invite the individual to feel the emotions and focus on the body sensations and images that emerge. As they tune in to the feeling-oriented, experiential room of the mind, I encourage them to disengage from the logical, analytical part of the mind that might otherwise prevent them from accessing the subconscious place of past memory events.

As the prayer recipient begins to engage the experiential part of the mind, my role is to ask feeling and belief questions and encourage them to let their mind go wherever it goes. (If you tune in to your triggers, your mind knows where to go.) I continue to ask the recipient how they are feeling, careful not to add or suggest emotions that the individual does not himself acknowledge, while asking them to tune into their body, any tension, tightness, rapid heartbeat, or shortness of breath.[1] Giving the individual the space to fully experience these sensations, without disengaging or suppressing, helps the individual to *feel* rather than *analyze* their emotions. As they engage emotionally with their own feelings, I reinforce the recipient's emotions in their own words and encourage them to revisit any memories that surface during this time. A healing-prayer dialogue between a prayer minister and a prayer recipient may go like this:

> **Prayer Minister**: *What feels bad or uncomfortable right now?*
>
> **Recipient**: *I feel anxious, sad and overwhelmed.*
>
> **Prayer Minister**: *Allow yourself to feel those anxious, sad and overwhelmed feelings. Is there anything else you feel emotionally or in your body. Do you see any images?*
>
> **Recipient**: *I also feel some frustration, loneliness and tightness in my chest.*
>
> **Prayer Minister**: *Just feel that frustration, loneliness, the tightness in your chest, along with the anxiety, sadness and overwhelmed feelings.*

During the opening prayer, and throughout our prayer sessions, it is common for images or memories to come into the person's mind. I encourage them to pay attention to whatever comes to their mind. Because the memories that emerge from their emotional triggers originate in the experiential part of their mind, they may not always make sense to the rational part of the mind. My goal, as a prayer minister and therapist, is to teach people to honor the experiential part of their mind and pay attention to and focus on their emotional triggers and images.

The subconscious mind is powerful and, on some level, it knows in which memories triggering emotions are rooted. Engaging the

---

[1] I use the resolved memory chart to help me to keep track of and record the healing process.

experiential room of the mind encourages people not to analyze where they think their mind *should* go, so it is free to go where it *needs* to go. This is ultimately important because disconnecting from the logical part of our mind helps us relinquish control of our analytical thinking so our emotional triggers can lead us to the past memory containers where our lie-based beliefs are rooted. Revisiting these memories, anchoring ourselves in them, and inviting Jesus to communicate truth to the lie-based beliefs stored in them are ultimately how we receive healing and breakthrough.[2] To help the prayer recipient anchor in a memory, I might ask a version of the following question:

"As a memory comes to mind, tell me how old you are, where you are and what is happening in the memory that emerges."

Let's take the example of how a 45-year-old man named Bobby might answer this question as he recalls a painful memory from his childhood. To help him *anchor* and receive healing in this painful memory, I would start by orienting him to:

Time at the point the memory took place. (*"Feel yourself in the memory as ten-year-old Bobby, not as the adult 45-year-old Bobby."*)

Place where the memory occurred. (*"Visualize yourself in the living room where your mom and dad are fighting."*)

Feelings that the individual experienced in the memory. (*"Allow yourself to experience the emotions from that memory: the scared and helpless feelings that you just expressed."*)

Beliefs at that time of life, usually childhood. (*"Does that feel true to ten-year-old Bobby in the memory?"*)[3]

Normally, when we think of a past memory, we do not "go" to the

---

[2] As the prayer minister, all I do during this process is intercede. After I help them to get in touch with their triggered emotions, connect with past memories and identify their lie-based beliefs, I simply ask Jesus to reveal what He wants them to know and to communicate His truth to bring freedom and release.

[3] His true belief is what feels true in the memory, even if it doesn't feel true now as an adult. For instance, a seven-year-old boy feels that the beating his father gave him with a razor strap was "his fault" and that he was a "bad boy."

memory; we just recall it. However, in the healing-prayer process, I want the prayer recipient to return to the memory and anchor themselves in it. I want them to tap into their feelings at the time the memory occurred and actively place themselves there. For instance, using the metaphor of our memory that appears like a movie reel, I do not want them to passively watch the memory replay as if on a screen; I want them to walk onto the set. I ask them (metaphorically) not to look in the window of the memory, but I invite them to walk in the door. I want them to tap into the feeling state at the time and place of the memory event. This helps them to access the embedded lie-based beliefs that need renewing.

ANCHORING THE RECIPIENT

Drawing upon what we have already learned throughout this book, it is critical to allow the recipient to fully feel, process and walk through their memories. In these instances, what *feels* true is more important than what is objectively true. As we said before, core beliefs bleed into our everyday life no matter what we intellectually believe to be true. During the healing-prayer session our goal is to help the prayer recipient decipher what feels true to them in the memory, and for this reason we help them anchor. Taking the example of 45-year-old Bobby from before, anchoring in a dialogue between a prayer minister and recipient may look like the following exchange.

Prayer Minister: *What do you feel in the memory as 10-year-old Bobby when mom and dad are fighting?*

Recipient: *I feel scared and helpless. I'm too little to do anything about it.*

Prayer Minister: *Why do you, as little Bobby, feel scared and helpless?*

Recipient: *I feel scared because I'm afraid my dad is going to hurt my mom and me. I feel helpless because it feels like I'm too little to do anything about it.*

Prayer Minister: *Is there anything else that happens as you look through this memory, any other feelings or thoughts?*

Recipient: *Yes, I'm feeling guilty.*

Prayer Minister: *Why is ten-year-old Bobby, with his parents fighting in the living room, feeling guilty?*

Recipient: *Because they are arguing about me.*

Prayer Minister: *Why does that make little Bobby feel guilty?*

Recipient: *It feels like it's my fault that they are fighting. I also feel like I'm bad, that there is something wrong with me. If I had been a better boy, they wouldn't fight as much and Dad would have stayed with us.*

Prayer Minister: *Is there anything else that happens or that you haven't looked at, felt or remembered as you look through this memory?*

Recipient: *No, I think that's everything.*

The *anchoring statement* in this exchange is found in the prayer minister's question "Why is ten-year-old Bobby, with his parents fighting in the living room, feeling guilty?" Using the recipient's own language, I am reminding him of his age (ten), his location (living room), and his feelings (scared, helpless, guilty). Anchoring him in the time frame, place and feelings brings the recipient to his belief: "*It's my fault that they are fighting; I'm bad; there is something wrong with me.*" The prayer minister's job is to help anchor the individual so they can connect with their painful, uncomfortable emotions and to set the stage for Jesus to reveal His truth.

As we continue to anchor him in the memory, the prayer minister should write down the recipient's feelings and beliefs that emerge so they can be repeated aloud to the recipient. As they are repeated, invite Jesus into the memory and, one by one, ask Jesus to communicate truth to each lie-based belief identified in the memory. Ask the prayer recipient to report what they *see, sense* or *hear*

Jesus communicate to them in the memory as they fully process through the painful emotions in the memory and identify their lie-based beliefs. For example,

> **Prayer Minister**: *Bobby, focus on your scared and helpless feelings, as you stay anchored in the memory. Jesus, what do You want little Bobby to know about feeling scared that his dad is going to hurt his mom and him?*

> **Recipient**: *I see Jesus standing between my dad and my mom and me.*

> **Prayer Minister**: *Bobby, what is Jesus communicating to you as little Bobby as He is standing between your dad and you and your mom?*

At this juncture, it is exceedingly important that the prayer minister should not make interpretations about what Jesus may be saying, but instead allow the prayer recipient to receive their communication directly from Jesus. This is where those of us who operate in the gifts of the Holy Spirit more comfortably may be tempted to intervene and offer our impression of what is happening. I implore you, *do not interject!* The goal of this healing session is to connect the recipient directly to God so they can hear His voice. Therefore, even if our interpretation may be correct, we will hinder the healing process by coming between God and the recipient if we intervene. Rest assured, the gifts of the Holy Spirit are operating, even if it looks different than you expect.

> **Recipient**: *I sense He is communicating to me that I am not helpless. I am even feeling bigger and empowered in the memory.*

> **Prayer Minister**: *Awesome. Now focus on the feelings of fear and the sense that something bad is going to happen. Bobby, what does Jesus want you to know about those beliefs?*
> **Recipient**: *He is saying that it is over now. I feel peace and a sense of light flooding the room and the fear is gone.*

Prayer Minister: *Bobby, does that feel true in the memory, that it's over now? Are you experiencing any fearful emotions in that memory? Are you feeling any sense of helplessness? What is Jesus communicating to you with the light flooding the memory picture?*

Recipient: *When the light flooded the memory it communicated to me that it is over now. The fear and helpless beliefs and feelings no longer feel true and the feelings of fear and helplessness are gone and replaced with peace.*

Note that I did not ask him if what Jesus communicated to him *was* true; I asked if it *felt* true in the memory?[*] Remember, most people already know the truth in the logical part of their mind, but we live and react from the triggered emotions of the experiential part of our mind. That is why we anchor the individual in the triggered emotions of their experience and memory: so we can invite Jesus to replace lie-based beliefs with His truth and replace negative emotions with His peace.

THE ROLE OF FREE WILL & CHOICE

As you work through memories as a prayer minister or recipient, remember that a key factor in a person's healing is their *free will*. A person's deepest will must be engaged in all aspects of the healing-prayer process. When I begin a session, I ask the recipient, "Are you willing to go to the memory and places connected to the emotions you are feeling?" If they are willing, I encourage them to fully tune into and feel their emotions, leave the present and allow their mind to go to the memory or memories where these feelings are rooted. It is the job of the prayer minister to bring the recipient into an awareness of opportunities to engage their will through acknowledging *points of decision* throughout the healing-prayer

---

[*]Bear in mind that we do, as believers, have the authority to judge all that is communicated from the Lord against Scripture and biblical principles. While you should not interpret Jesus' words or actions for the individual, you may judge all truth revealed from Jesus in memory with its alignment to biblical truth.

process. While deciding to receive healing-prayer is the first decision point, there are many more to make during and after the healing process. For example, once they make the decision to receive healing prayer, they can move forward as quickly or as slowly as they would like. God has created us with free will and gives the choice to engage in the healing process (to feel, to remember, to release anger, to break vows, etc.); each step is ours to make.

Several years ago, I worked with a Christian woman who had heard me teach on Mind Renewing Healing Prayer and understood the process. After talking to her briefly, we quickly moved into a 50-minute healing-prayer session. As we began to pray, she immediately dropped into two childhood sexual abuse memories that had greatly wounded her sense of self and negatively impacted her life for decades. She was very willing to receive and the Lord quickly and dramatically healed memories that had haunted her for 50 years. It was glorious to behold.

Because not all participants are so fully engaged and willing, healing does not always occur this quickly, but often it does. When recipients are emotionally shut down, I have to spend more time helping them to choose to work through their defenses that keep them from moving forward in the healing process. There are many choices one must make throughout the Mind Renewing Healing Prayer process. The recipient must choose to:

1. *Feel* their emotions.
2. *Let down* their defenses and work through their resistance.
3. *Anchor* themselves and stay anchored in the memories that emerge.
4. *Release anger* and *forgive.*
5. *Renounce vows, curses* and *judgments.*
6. *Choose to receive* the Lord's healing communication.

Part of engaging the recipient's will involves addressing any hindrances or blocks that may slow or stop the process. In many instances, you may need to lead the recipient through breaking or renouncing vows, curses and judgments as they work through the memories that emerge. Additionally, you may need to encourage them to release resentment and vengeful emotions (anger, bitterness, hatred, resentment, etc.) to the Lord and forgive those who have hurt them. We will deal more with these specific processes in the following chapters, but for now bear in mind that the healing process is not complete for an individual until these hindrances or blockages are addressed.

CONCLUSION

Once you have walked someone through the Mind Renewing Healing Prayer process, have them "feel through" the memory again to make sure it is fully calm, the negative emotions are resolved and the memory is filled with peace. Remember to check that all the lie-based beliefs, emotions and body sensations that have been identified during the session are fully resolved. If there is not 100 percent total peace, have them focus on the remaining triggered emotions to determine if there's anything that you have missed in the memory or if any other memories come to the surface. As time allows, feel free to go through the same process with as many memories as surface during a session. When a memory appears to be healed, revisit the initial memory to ensure it no longer triggers negative feelings, sensations or reactions. When all the memories that have emerged are resolved, return to the trigger where you started. If it is indeed healed and full of peace, then you are finished with your healing session.

PRACTICE & PRINCIPLES

PRACTICE

1. **Open in prayer** - Invite the Holy Spirit. Have the recipient close their eyes, feel uncomfortable emotions, body sensations and focus on any images that may be present.

2. **Ask the recipient** - "What emotions and body sensations are you feeling now as I'm praying?"

3. **Encourage recipient** - Ask them to disengage from the *analytical* part of their mind and tune into the *experiential*, feeling part of their mind.

4. **Record** - The prayer minister should take note of feelings, body sensations, images and beliefs, vows, curses and judgments, charting them on the *resolved memory chart*.

5. **Reinforce emotions and bodily sensations to the recipient** - Encourage them to allow their mind to go to any memories that emerge. Emphasize they should refrain from engaging the logical part of their mind and just *feel*.

6. **Emphasize free will and choice** - Bring them into an awareness of their *points of decision*.

7. **Anchor the recipient** - Remind the prayer recipient to stay *anchored* in the memory.

8. **Invite Jesus** - Ask Him to communicate truth to the lie-based beliefs you have identified in memory.

9. **Confirm resolution** - Feel through the memory or series of memories using the above principles with the prayer recipient until it is 100 percent peaceful, calm and resolved.

PRINCIPLES

Example of a completed Resolved Memory Chart using Bobby's healing journey.

PRESENTING EMOTIONS	MEMORY PICTURES	LIES BELIEVED/ OBJECTIONS	TRUTH RECEIVED
• Scared • Helpless • Guilty	• 10-years-old • Parents fighting • Living room	• Dad is going to hurt me and mom • I am too little to do anything about it • It's my fault they are fighting • I'm bad • Something is wrong with me • If I had been a better boy they wouldn't fight as much and dad wouldn't have left	• I see Jesus standing between mom and me • I am not helpless • I am feeling empowered • It's over now • I feel peace and a sense of light flooding the room • Fear is gone • I feel totally peaceful, calm and the memory is resolved

CHAPTER 10

FREE WILL AND CHOICE

"A man convinced against his will is of the same opinion still."[1]

"And the Lord God commanded the man, saying, 'Of every tree of the garden you may freely eat; but of the tree of the knowledge of good and evil you shall not eat, for in the day that you eat of it you shall surely die.'"
(GENESIS 2:16-17, NKJV)

HEALING PRINCIPLE: To pursue one's healing journey is to take the road less traveled. It involves going against the grain of our natural desire to avoid dealing with pain, conflict and the tough issues of life. The good news is that the benefits of pursuing our personal healing journey far outweigh just living a mundane life of avoidance. As we diligently pursue our healing journey and our mind is renewed, our quality of life dramatically improves. We begin to experience increased levels of confidence and peace of mind as we align ourselves with God, putting ourselves in a place to walk in our true destiny, life purpose and calling.

---

[1]*How to Win Friends and Influence People,* Dale Carnegie.http://www.goodreads.com-quotes/96854-a-man-convinced-against-his-will-is-of-the-same

A key factor in the Mind Renewing Healing Prayer process is understanding the role of the prayer recipient's free will and choice. In *Mind Renewing Healing Prayer*, nothing happens that the prayer recipient does not want to happen at the deepest level of their psyche. A key to effective healing-prayer ministry is that we must learn how to engage the prayer recipient's will at the deepest level. We see in Genesis 2 that God put the tree in the Garden of Eden to forever anchor free will and choice into humanity. The concept comes from God and we should recognize its importance when we minister.

When I meet with a client, I explain the Mind Renewing Healing Prayer process to them and provide some articles I have written on the subject. The concepts usually make sense to them. My goal in doing this is to see if they are interested in engaging their deepest will in the Mind Renewing Healing Prayer process. I may know what I think they need, and often I am right, but it is completely up to them. The process won't work unless they're fully engaged.

THREE LEVELS OF ENGAGEMENT

I find that there are three levels of engagement among people who come for Mind Renewing Healing Prayer. The first is the *disinterested*. Some people are just not interested in engaging in the process. Occasionally, I will hear about a healing-prayer minister who pressures people to engage in this type of prayer ministry. I do not pressure people to engage. Many people come to see me to do this work, usually because they have heard of its effectiveness through someone else's testimony. I present it to them as an option to deal with their symptoms and presenting problem. If I think it is appropriate, I usually tell them that I believe it will also be the most effective and helpful option for them. But I always respect their free will and choice, as the Lord does with us.

The next level is the *verbally committed*. There are those who say they are willing to enter into their healing journey but who do not deeply will to do so. These are people who say they want to be healed and engage in the Mind Renewing Healing Prayer process, but choose to talk instead of entering into a healing-prayer session. Or they pray but they are continually stuck or blocked in the process. *Their deepest will is not fully engaged.* We need to work with their resistance. Often, we can help them to engage more deeply, but the prayer minister cannot engage another's deepest will for them. Just like the rich young ruler, we all must choose.

The next level is the *totally committed*, those who jump in with both feet and lean into their healing journey. When they arrive for a healing session, they quickly take ownership and proactively choose to move quickly into healing prayer. They move into the wounded places of their past, receive a revelation of His truth and walk in His peace and overcoming! They obviously reap the greatest results.

JESUS, FREE WILL AND CHOICE

"Now as He was going out on the road, one came running, knelt before Him, and asked Him, "Good Teacher, what shall I do that I may inherit eternal life?" So Jesus said to him, "Why do you call Me good? No one is good but One, that is, God. You know the commandments: 'Do not commit adultery,' 'Do not murder,' 'Do not steal,' 'Do not bear false witness,' 'Do not defraud,' 'Honor your father and your mother.'" And he answered and said to Him, "Teacher, all these things I have kept from my youth." Then Jesus, looking at him, loved him, and said to him, "One thing you lack: Go your way, sell whatever you have and give to the poor, and you will have treasure in heaven; and come, take up the cross, and follow Me." But he was sad at this word, and went away sorrowful, for he had great possessions."

(MARK 10:17-22, NKJV)

In this passage, Jesus addresses a wealthy, influential young man who was probably a leader in his synagogue and community. Morally, he was a good man; he followed the law and, unlike many of the Jewish religious leaders at the time, he had a revelation of who Jesus was. It appeared to the disciples that he would be a good candidate for leadership in the new sect of Christ followers.

Instead, Jesus looks at the man and *He challenged him to engage the deepest part of his will and to choose to follow Him.* In the same way, we must choose to engage our deepest will, to feel, remember, and hear the voice of Jesus during the Mind Renewing Healing Prayer process. Just like the rich young ruler, the truth of our condition may be painful to hear, but if we will submit our hearts to the lordship of Jesus, we will step into our healing, victory and walk boldly into our destiny and life purpose.

Sick people want to healed, but sometimes in order to be well they need surgery. Some are not willing to undergo the needed surgery required to heal their wounded heart. The rich young ruler was a law-observer and a good, moral man. It appears he wanted to be a part of what God was doing through Jesus. Why then would Jesus be so hard on him? Why didn't He cut him a little slack and give him some grace?

But He answered and said to the one who told Him,

"Who is My mother and who are My brothers?" And He stretched out His hand toward His disciples and said, "Here are My mother and My brothers! For whoever does the will of My Father in heaven is My brother and sister and mother."

(MATTHEW 12:48-50, NKJV)

To whom much is given, much is expected. I assume God was not angry with the rich young ruler, quite the contrary. I assume God had spectacular plans just waiting to be unfolded into his life, just like He did for the disciples and us today. This is actually similar to the struggle with which so many of us wrestle. However, the young ruler was not willing to risk his wealth and earthly status to do so. In other words, *he wanted to be better, but he was unwilling to undergo the needed surgery.* To be a Christ follower requires faith and obedience.

*"He who finds his life will lose it, and he who loses his life for
My sake will find it."*

(MATTHEW 10:39, NKJV)

The rich young ruler was not willing to *lose his life* as the disciples
had. They walked away from their fishing, tax collecting and various
vocations to follow Jesus. Often, the more we have in terms of earthly possessions and status, the harder it is to let go of our lives. There
is a risk when we radically turn to Christ. The apostle Paul had been
a rising star in his day but lost his position in the religious hierarchy,
in which he was destined for stardom, when he chose to follow Jesus.
After he abandoned his bright future for Christ, his reputation and
hopes for future advancement in the Pharisaical system were dashed.

*"though I also might have confidence in the flesh. If anyone else
thinks he may have confidence in the flesh, I more so: circumcised
the eighth day, of the stock of Israel, of the tribe of Benjamin,
a Hebrew of the Hebrews; concerning the law, a Pharisee; concerning zeal, persecuting the church; concerning the righteousness which is in the law, blameless. But what things were gain to
me, these I have counted loss for Christ. Yet indeed I also count
all things loss for the excellence of the knowledge of Christ Jesus my Lord, for whom I have suffered the loss of all things, and
count them as rubbish, that I may gain Christ."*

(PHILIPPIANS 3:4-8, NKJV)

Being fully released into our destiny requires major engagement of our will. There are issues in our lives, like the rich young
ruler and Paul, that the Lord will reveal. It is our responsibility to
deal with them in order to make progress in our healing journey
and, ultimately, to move on and find our God-given destiny. If we
choose and engage well, we will, like Paul, find all other things to
be worthless in comparison to gaining Christ.

*"Behold, I stand at the door, and knock: if any man hear my
voice, and open the door, I will come in to him, and will sup*

with him, and he with me."

(REVELATION 3:20, KJV)

The Lord is invitational and knocks on the door of our heart in order to engage our will. In the same way, Mind Renewing Healing Prayer must be invitational by design. When I administer healing prayer, I look for every opportunity to invite recipients to engage their wills in session. Here are some of the big and small decisions prayer recipients can make during session.

1. Choose to engage in beginning the healing-prayer process.
2. Choose to feel their emotions.
3. Choose to feel body memory and sensations.
4. Choose to remember dissociated and repressed memory (for the deeply traumatized).
5. Choose to listen internally to their resistance and lie-based beliefs that prevent them from moving forward.
6. Choose to find the guardian lies and move through the blocks, walls and barriers preventing them from seeing, remembering, feeling and hearing Jesus.
7. Choose to hear Jesus in the Mind Renewing Healing Prayer process.[2]
8. Choose to feel, express and release their anger to the Lord and to forgive from their heart.
9. Choose to break and renounce vows, curses, judgments, generational curses and soul ties.
10. Choose to repent and renounce former occult, New Age, and false religious experiences.
11. Choose to confess and repent of sin.

---

[2]Some people may argue that they cannot hear from God. In my experience, the reason people do not hear God is usually anger at God, which they may or may not initially recognize. Another reason is a shame lie; they may believe, "I'm not worthy enough to hear God."

12. Choose to feel and release grief and mourning to the Lord.

It is the prayer minister's job to help the recipient choose to engage their will at the deepest level. Just because one is willing to participate in the healing-prayer process does not guarantee they will receive the healing they need. There is a process of engagement of one's will. This is done when the prayer minister brings the recipient to the *points of decision* throughout the prayer process. It is up to the healing-prayer minister to understand their role in healing the ministry recipient by helping them choose to receive the healing they need. Ultimately, we do not force them to choose; it is the responsibility of the prayer recipient to make their choices.

BRUSSELS SPROUTS

Thomas Friedman, a *New York Times* OP-ED Columnist, wrote a story several years back in reference to nuclear proliferation. I think it has a profound truth in regards to engagement of the will in the Mind Renewing Healing Prayer process.

> *In his book The Ideas That Conquered the World, Michael Mandelbaum tells a story about a young girl who is eating dinner at a friend's house and her friend's mother asks her if she likes Brussels sprouts. "Yes, of course," the girl says. "I like brussels sprouts." After dinner, though, the mother notices that the girl hasn't eaten a single sprout. "I thought you liked Brussels sprouts," the mother said. "I do," answered the girl, "but not enough to actually eat them."*[3]

During the healing-prayer session, there are those prayer recipients who are willing to participate and we enter into the Mind Renewing Healing Prayer process itself. What happens at times, which is common, is that the process is blocked or shut down, usually from the healing-prayer recipient's own inner ambivalence

---

[3]Thomas Friedman, Brussel Sprouts. http://www.nytimes.com/2005/05/11/opinion/11friedman.html?_r=1&.

or resistance. This manifests in a few ways. It may be that during prayer no memory comes to mind, the person experiences sudden emotional shut down, or they only want to discuss a memory instead of processing through it. This is where the metaphor comes into play. The little girl liked Brussels sprouts in the same way that some approach our healing journey. They may verbally commit to Mind Renewing Healing Prayer, but like the little girl, they do not want their healing enough to go through the steps of tasting, chewing, swallowing and digesting.

THE WIZARD OF OZ

[For being as he is] a man of two minds (hesitating, dubious, irresolute), [he is] unstable and unreliable and uncertain about everything [he thinks, feels, decides].

(JAMES 1:8, AMPC)

Another example I use with clients is the *Wizard of Oz*. In the movie, Dorothy is trying to see the Wizard. When she finally meets him, she finds that behind the Wizard's noise, smoke, fire and bluster, there is only a *little guy behind a curtain* who is running the show. Our deepest will is our little guy behind the curtain, our internal decision-maker self. This is what I mean by posing questions to the inner mind. When one's deepest self is on board with one's outer mind, then we quickly move forward toward mind renewal and healing in the Mind Renewing Healing Prayer process.

THE ROAD LESS TRAVELED

In the next chapter, we will discuss hindrances and blocks to the Mind Renewing Healing Prayer process. But generally speaking, the reason most people are stuck in session has to do with some variations of *pain avoidance*. In his classic book, *The Road Less Traveled*, M. Scott Peck talks about the fact that most of us do not take the road less traveled. We take the easier road, the road of least resistance. For the most part, we humans are pain avoiders.

To pursue one's healing journey is to take the road less traveled. It involves going against the grain of our natural desire to avoid dealing with pain, conflict and the tough issues of life. The good news is that the benefits of pursuing our personal healing journey far outweigh just living a mundane life of avoidance. As we diligently pursue our healing journey, our mind is renewed and our quality of life dramatically improves. We begin to experience increased levels of confidence and peace of mind as we align ourselves with God, putting ourselves in a place to walk in our true destiny, life purpose and calling.

WE LISTEN TO ADVICE; WE OBEY PAIN

The one thing that tends to motivate us to engage our wills is pain. We have pain because of our choices, the choices of others or things that happen outside of our control. Often, we are reaping the harvest of what we have sown by decisions we have made or not made. Earlier in the chapter, I introduced the three levels of engagement in Mind Renewing Healing Prayer: the *disinterested,* the *verbally committed* and *the totally committed.* The third category is simply the engaged or the *totally committed*: those who have totally engaged their will are highly motivated for healing.

Obviously, this is where the most motivated people effectively work and find breakthrough. When I work with people coming in for healing prayer or therapy, these are the ones who receive optimal healing and overcome. They experience little or no resistance to moving forward on their healing journey as their wills are fully engaged.

DOWN THE DOG'S THROAT

Years ago, I heard a trauma therapist give a great analogy in dealing with traumatic memories. The same principle applies to dealing with healing-prayer sessions. He asked, if a dog attacked you, bit your hand and wouldn't let go, what would you do? Most of us would obviously try to pull our hand out of the attacking dog's mouth and flee the situation. However, that is not what you should do. If you tried to pull away from the dog, he would continue to attack; the greatest damage would be done to the person who tried to pull away. Surprisingly, the best decision in the case of attack would be to push your hand down the dog's throat in order to hit its gag reflex.

Dogs put up great resistance as you pull away, but almost no resistance as you push your hand inward, down their throat. I know what you are thinking. Who in their right mind, when bitten by a dog, would push their hand farther down a dog's throat? It certainly wouldn't be my first thought. But if you ram your hand down the dog's throat, you hit their gag reflex, temporarily cutting off their air supply; likely, you would be released and the dog would run away. Human nature wants to run away from and avoid pain at all costs. That is a common theme in the Mind Renewing Healing Prayer process. We all want to be healed, but we don't want to feel the pain. *However, if we will choose to go deep inside the memory, instead of trying to pull away from it, we will ultimately be released.* This manifests in freedom and breakthrough.

Kim's Story

I once worked with a woman named Kim. When she came for healing sessions, she was deeply wounded and in distress. She was very emotionally stirred up as memories started to emerge after watching a movie about a sexual abuse victim. It was recommended that she come to do some healing sessions with me. Initially she came filled with anxiety but with great resolve, willed to press into her healing journey. Her inner mind knew the trauma that she had undergone in her childhood, even though she was not fully aware of it when she initially came into my office. As we began our sessions after some initial resistance, she quickly engaged her deepest will in the Mind Renewing Healing Prayer process. She chose to go to her deeply buried and dissociated traumatic memories from her childhood. I explained to her the concept of engaging her deepest will and that if she would choose to engage deeply in the healing-prayer process, the greater the breakthrough she was more likely to experience. She chose, week after week, to go to the places of her severe physical, emotional and sexual abuse trauma. For the first time in her life she began to experience tremendous breakthroughs in her interpersonal relationships. Her sense of self-worth greatly improved as her shame, fear and powerlessness disappeared. She chose to go down the throat of the dog, so to speak, into the depths of her being, to her painful, dissociated, sexual trauma memories that were now leaking and robbing her of the abundant life God had intended for her. Her healing and transformation were glorious to behold as she journeyed with God in my office to the depths of her trauma, working through, confronting and laying to rest her lie-based thinking that resulted in dramatic breakthrough, healing and peace.

CHAPTER 11

HINDRANCES AND BLOCKS IN THE MIND RENEWING HEALING PRAYER PROCESS

"My people are destroyed for lack of knowledge; because you [the priestly nation] have rejected knowledge, I will also reject you that you shall be no priest to Me; seeing you have forgotten the law of your God, I will also forget your children."
(HOSEA 4:6, AMPC)

HEALING PRINCIPLE: In life, far too often, we do not grasp the knowledge and revelation that the Bible imparts to us, especially with regard to healing. If we do not seek what Scripture says about healing, we will be vulnerable, uncovered and our lives will be greatly diminished. We must do it God's way, following His principles in order to receive the full measure of His healing, blessing and breakthrough.

When I purchase something, I do not always read the owner's manual. I've learned that, when I don't, I often miss important details until I go back and read the instructions. The cost is far greater for not reading and applying the Bible, our heavenly owner's manual. Unfortunately, we miss the full measure of the healing God wants to impart to us until we do it the way He has instructed. This chapter discusses some of the hindrances to our healing that I have discovered over the years and how to read and apply the Bible's instructions to break through that which would impede our freedom.

We live in a culture where the microwave, Instagram and the 15-second video clip have made instant gratification and overstimulation commonplace. The problem is, that trickles into every area of our life; we are often looking for instant gratification, a sound bite or another quick fix for our emotional pain. We would rather post a pretty picture than admit to our problems. We lack the patience and resolve to work through our issues.

> *"Do not be deceived, God is not mocked; for whatever a man sows, that he will also reap. For he who sows to his flesh will of the flesh reap corruption, but he who sows to the Spirit will of the Spirit reap everlasting life. And let us not grow weary while doing good, for in due season we shall reap if we do not lose heart."*
>
> (GALATIANS 6:7-9, NKJV)

As much as we would like to, sowing and reaping is a principle of life we cannot escape. Learning to delay gratification and cope with pain in healthy ways is part of the maturation process. In order to do this, we must engage our will and learn to work through the hindrances and blocks that keep us from wholeness. In a healing-prayer session, we must not only outwardly choose to move forward, but we need to deal with our inner defenses and engage our will at the deepest level. When I am counseling with and ministering to a client, I ask them at the beginning of a session if they want to engage in healing prayer or do something else that day. I let them choose to engage in a therapy session, whether or not they are open to being ministered to with healing prayer. Everyone who comes to Meadows Healing Prayer Center understands that they are coming for the sole purpose of receiving Mind Renewing Healing Prayer, but I verbalize this to reinforce their choice and to give them an opportunity to engage in the sowing and reaping of their healing.

ANGER

In my experience, there are five things that block, hinder or slow a Mind Renewing Healing Prayer session. The number one block to healing is unresolved anger. Anger, bitterness, resentment, hatred and vengeful emotions experienced in the memories during the healing-prayer process are normal. It is normal to feel some type of anger reaction when we have experienced hurt, mistreatment or abuse. If someone says they do not feel deep anger, resentment or hatred when they have been terribly wounded, I assume they may have deeply buried it, suppressed it and may not yet be in touch with it. Emotions need to be felt, expressed and released to the Lord. However, one's unwillingness to release anger emotions can stop the flow of a healing session. In memory, the recipient must express and then release their anger from the deepest part of their being to Jesus.

> *"In your anger do not sin: Do not let the sun go down while you are still angry, and do not give the devil a foothold."*
>
> (EPHESIANS 4:26-27, NIV)

Being angry when we are wronged is a normal human reaction. Still, the Bible tells us not to sin in our anger, lest we give the devil a foothold. If there is anger in a person's memory, healing usually does not occur until it is released by the prayer recipient. Guardian lies can hold one's anger in place and block the healing process from moving forward. A revelation of truth from the Lord is needed in order to move forward toward healing. *Guardian lies* are beliefs such as "The anger protects me," or "I would be vulnerable without it." They require a revelation of truth from Jesus. The revelation is needed in order for the person to choose to release the lie and move more deeply into their healing. Sometimes people have unknowingly buried their anger and resentment or feel guilty for being angry in the first place. They do not need my permission to be angry, but as the prayer minister I "give" them permission to feel and express their emotions. Once they are in touch with their emotions, I can lead them through a releasing prayer in which they can express and release their anger to Jesus and allow Him to take it.

> *Lord, I am very angry at my father who never showed up for any of my football games. I feel angry, bitter, and resentful that he didn't care enough about me enough to come to my games and that his work was more important. Lord, I give this anger, bitterness and resentment to You, and I ask You to take it and to heal me. I choose to forgive and release my father in Jesus' name.*

VOWS, CURSES AND JUDGMENTS

Another block to the healing process is the presence of *vows, curses and judgments*. I am always listening for these when I am in session. I deal with them in a similar fashion as I help the prayer recipient process through the memory event. They must choose to confess to God and out loud to another believer and renounce any vows, curses and judgments or it will hinder the flow of healing.

My definition of a vow is simply an inner decision made to survive emotionally, psychologically or even physically during a time of pain, abuse or distress. Vows tend to be rooted in childhood and reinforced throughout our lives. People do not tend to recognize them for what they are. They are made often outside of our conscious awareness or without understanding the full significance of what we are doing. Vows tend to evolve into unhealthy patterns of coping that are often disruptive to healthy interpersonal relationships and living. One reason it is important to recognize the role of the vows is because demonic powers can strengthen and reinforce our internal agreements that are not in line with biblical truths and reality. They do not have the authority to violate our deepest will, but they can keep us in bondage. For example, a person who has undergone abuse may intellectually know the biblical truth "I am fearfully and wonderfully made" but still may deep down believe "I am bad, shameful and unworthy." The vows protect and reinforce the lies; the enemy can dwell in these lies until they receive a revelation of truth.

An example of a vow protecting these lies might be if I make a decision to not trust, feel or remember. This may manifest in a thought such as, *People can't be trusted so I am on my own.* The vow reinforces the lie and holds the lie-based stronghold in place.

Part of breaking and renouncing a vow includes breaking all demonic ties to it. This is not difficult to do. We *agreed* to believe a lie, usually in ignorance, and now we are just *disagreeing* with and renouncing it. In doing so, by engaging our will, we are also renouncing any connection to the demonic, any help that may have given us, or any negative fruit that came as a result of it in the name of Jesus.

My observation is that demons reinforce what we have already decided in our hearts. They cannot violate our deepest will, so, instead, they come into agreement with what we have chosen in our hearts. Unfortunately, sometimes what we have chosen comes from demonic deception. They are distorters and deceivers. That is why it is so beautiful to see the Lord communicate truth to our lie-based thinking in memory. It is a very liberating event. When I am leading a person through breaking a vow, I ask them to pray out loud after me in the following way.

> *"Lord, I confess the vow or decision I made_____ (e.g.; to not trust, feel or remember). Lord, I also renounce that vow and sever all demonic ties with that vow or decision in Jesus' name. Lord, I also ask that You would restore what was stolen and help me to trust again in healthy ways, to feel and express my emotions, and remember things I need to remember, address and process in Jesus' name."*

A curse is not unlike a vow, except in who initiates it. I define a curse as something hurtful or demeaning that was spoken or implied by a person in authority over another person, usually in their childhood. These people are primarily parents, as well as grandparents, caretakers, babysitters, teachers or any person who has some level of authority. A curse could be "I wish you were never born," or "You will never amount to anything; you are just like your father." Similar to breaking a vow, curses must be broken as well. Vows of agreement are often subtly made in agreement with a curse. I lead prayer recipients to break the curses over their lives by simply leading them to say the following prayer.

> "I break the curse that was spoken over me_____
> (e.g.; that I was not wanted by my mother). I renounce that curse my mother spoke and implied over me by her words, actions and behaviors, and I break any vows of agreement I made with it. I sever all demonic ties with that curse and any vows of agreement with it in Jesus' name! I ask You to restore what has been stolen from me in the name of Jesus. I choose to live fully and completely in who You created me to be and to completely embrace the life You've given me, in Jesus' name!"

Judgments operate like vows and curses; however, they are pronouncements we make against other people, typically one who has wounded or offended us in the past. We may judge individuals or types of people based on their race, religion, denomination, sex, political persuasion, culture or socioeconomic status, etc. We often judge people we do not like or of whom we are jealous. For example, wounded people may judge their parents by labeling them a "bad mother" or "bad father."

> "Judge not, that you be not judged. For with the judgment you pronounce you will be judged, and with the measure you use it will be measured to you."
>
> (MATTHEW 7:1-2, ESV)

It is easy to judge others when we are wronged and feel justified in doing so, but Scripture gives us a stern warning against it: *judge not, that you be not judged.* It is also easy to be self-righteous and to think arrogantly that we have superior knowledge and that anyone who doesn't feel or believe like we do must be wrong. Like curses and vows, we must pray to renounce judgements.

> *I confess the judgment I made_____ (e.g., that my mother was a terrible mother and that I would never be like her). I renounce this judgment and sever all ties of darkness with that in Jesus' name. I choose to let You be the judge and ask that You would help me to establish healthy boundaries and to forgive and love my mother in Jesus' name.*

DISSOCIATION, REPRESSION AND DEFENSE MECHANISMS

The third category that produces blocks and hindrances includes dissociation, repression and other protective defense mechanisms. We can get stuck in a Mind Renewing Healing Prayer session if we do not understand dissociation and how to effectively deal with it. Dissociation primarily occurs when children are traumatized and abused sexually and physically. It can also occur when they go through severe emotional and physical pain, medical procedures and surgeries. As we discussed previously, dissociation is the defensive choice that happens outside of one's conscious awareness and most commonly occurs to children under the age of five or six. The mind has the ability to protect the child by dissociating painful memories, emotions and physical pain, totally out of one's conscious awareness. God has put within the brain the ability to protect us by disconnecting from painful memories, emotions, and body memories.

One of the reasons we must deal with our dissociation is that dissociative barriers tend to "leak" over time. I observe this especially in the women I work with who have been sexually traumatized in their childhood. In my experiences, their dissociative barriers typically start leaking between the ages of thirty-five and forty-five. This is not always the case, but very often it is. Men's dissociative barriers are also more likely to begin leaking as they grow older. They typically are more resistant to talking about their abuse and telling their story because they perceive it as threatening to their ego or sense of manhood. I tell both men and women that it takes guts to address their abuse and to begin their healing journey.

Dissociation is meant to help us survive painful, traumatic life events, but it is not meant to be a permanent solution. It is similar to undergoing physical shock, but it may last for decades instead of hours. What's important to remember about dissociation is that it's only meant to help us survive until we are old enough or ready to assimilate and process the trauma. On the far end of the continuum of dissociation, DID (dissociative identity disorder) can develop, which was previously known as multiple personality disorder.

UNCONFESSED SIN

Unconfessed sin is the least common reason that someone would get stuck in the healing-prayer process, but it is also a hindrance to healing. At times, it completely shuts down a Mind Renewing Healing Prayer session. For instance, if someone is living in blatant, sexual sin, the solution is simple. The antidote is confession and repentance to God and another believer. When that occurs, the block is removed and the healing process continues and moves forward. There is also a need to repent and renounce our involvement for spiritual sin, which includes current or past involvement in the occult, New Age, Christian cults or involvement in other false religions. This involvement needs to be confessed, renounced and repented. Below is an example of how I lead a recipient in a prayer of confession, repentance and renunciation.

> *Lord, I confess that I participated in_____(e.g., the occult practice of Wicca). I repent and ask Your forgiveness. I renounce any and all involvement in Wicca, and I command all demonic spirits to leave my presence, never to return*

or send replacements in Jesus' name. I am thankful that Your blood covers me and cleanses me from all unrighteousness. I ask You to fill me anew with Your Holy Spirt and to restore sevenfold what the enemy has stolen from me, in Jesus' name.

"Men do not despise a thief, if he steals to satisfy his soul when he is hungry; But if he be found, he shall restore sevenfold; he shall give all the substance of his house."

(PROVERBS 6:30-31, KJV)

GENERATIONAL CURSES

The final hindrance I see to Mind Renewing Healing Prayer is generational curses. We see biblical evidence for generational curses in Exodus 20:5-6.

"For I, the Lord your God, am a jealous God, visiting the iniquity of the fathers upon the children to the third and fourth generations of those who hate Me, but showing mercy to thousands, to those who love Me and keep My commandments."

(EXODUS 20:5-6, NKJV)

There are times when we need to break the generational curses that have not been broken or renounced in order to walk in maximized freedom. The gifts of the Holy Spirit, specifically *word of knowledge* and *discerning of spirits,* are always available to us in the healing-prayer process. We must tune into the operation of the gifts of the Holy Spirit and not be ignorant in regards to their manifestation and operation. God has provided them for our good and to accelerate the healing process. I find this relates to generational curses when the Holy Spirit gives discernment to or prompts the prayer minister or prayer recipient of any spiritual darkness present as a result of previous generations opening the door through their sin. As a prayer minister I do not suggest it but I may ask questions exploring the previous generations. Or the prayer recipient may say something like, "I see a picture of my grandmother. She also had a history of depression and low self-esteem. She was adopted and always struggled with rejection and abandonment, like I do." I may ask them if they feel there is any generational demonic activity that needs to be broken and, if they are willing, I will lead them in a prayer to break and renounce any generational curses.

In this case, the Holy Spirit may be giving us *discernment* not only about a series of memories that need healing but also generational issues in the family line. Remember, the Lord wants His people to be saved, healed and delivered far more than we do. It's very clear in 1 John 3:8 that Jesus came to "destroy the works of the devil." He wants to remove the generational curses, the legal right the enemy may have to dwell in your generational family system.

There are times that deliverance from generational curses is needed in order for healing to take place. It takes a spiritually discerning ear to determine when it is needed. As a prayer minister, you will be far more effective as you cultivate the gifts of the Holy Spirit in the context of a Mind Renewing Healing Prayer session. I find this is especially relevant when there has been personal or family involvement in New Age, witchcraft, occult or Freemasonry, along with other familial patterns of sin and brokenness throughout the generations. The Bible says that Jesus became a curse for us on the cross (see Galatians 3:13). In other words, Jesus not only bore our sins, wounds, sickness, infirmities and pain, but He also became a curse for us in order to bear and break the generational curses that gave the enemy entrance into our family systems. When Jesus died for our sin on the cross and shed His precious blood, the enemy's legal right to cling to us through the generational sins from our lineage was broken. It is our job to appropriate what He has already accomplished on the cross.

Prayer to break generational curses: *I confess the sins and patterns of living of my ancestors_____.*
I plant the cross of Jesus between my parents, grandparents and previous generations and between myself, my children, grandchildren and future generations. I confess and repent for

*the sins and patterns of living of my ancestors (e.g., and spe-
cifically my mother's fear, worry, panic, terror and anxiety). I
declare You have not given us a spirit of fear but one of love,
power and a sound mind. I announce to the spirits of darkness
that You, Jesus, became a curse for us on the cross, according
to Galatians 3:13, so that we do not have to bear these curses. With the sword of the Spirit I sever, renounce and break
these curses. I command all demonic spirits who have had legal
ground in my life to go and leave me, my family and future
generations, never to return or send replacements, in Jesus'
name! I now ask for the blessings of the generations, everything that You have intended for me and my family from the
foundation of the world, according to Ephesians 2:10, to be
released fully and completely now in Jesus' name!*

DEMONIZATION AND INNER HEALING

While inner healing is not deliverance, it is often a byproduct of
Mind Renewing Healing Prayer. It is not deliverance in the sense
that we are not directly going after the demonic to cast them out.
Instead, Mind Renewing Healing Prayer goes deeper, to the root
of the problem. Dr. Smith, the founder of Theophostic, says that
"The problem isn't the flies; it's the outhouse." In deliverance ministry my observation is that sometimes they go after the demon, for
instance "fear," instead of the root cause of the demon's presence.
If you try to cast out a spirit of fear (the rat), instead of praying
into the emotion of fear leading to the memory where the fear beliefs are rooted (the garbage can), we often miss the issue. Deliverance often takes place without ever directly addressing the demon
that may dwell in that belief in the memory. Unfortunately, many
of us do not get the complete breakthrough that God intends for
His children because we do not understand this. Mind Renewing
Healing Prayer helps get to the root of the problem, when the origin is lie-based thinking.

Discerning of spirits is a gift and is not limited to discerning
the presence of the demonic. At times, I sense the Holy Spirit or

angelic ministering spirits in my sessions. I believe they're always at work in my Mind Renewing Healing Prayer sessions. I often sense what the Lord is doing in a healing session through the operation of the gifts of the Holy Spirit. Consider the story of Elijah in 2 Kings 6:8-23. While the Syrian army surrounded them, Elijah saw a massive, greater angelic army surrounding them and warring on their behalf. His servant was afraid, and Elijah asked the Lord to open his spiritual eyes, to see into the spiritual realm. God opened the servant's eyes, and he saw the incredible angel army surrounding them. His fear left and they were miraculously delivered. I highly recommend praying the following prayer to grow in discernment of spirits:

> *Lord, open our spiritual eyes to see and discern what You are doing, to operate in the gifts of the Spirit, especially discerning of spirits. Help me to sense what the Holy Spirit is doing and to sense the presence and working of angelic beings. Also, help me to discern when and how demonic entities are present, what legal right they have to be there, and how to destroy the works of the devil in my life and in those I minster to in Jesus' name!*

I believe utilizing the gifts of the Holy Spirit are essential in the Mind Renewing Healing Prayer process. (I am planning in the future to write more on the operation of the gifts of the Holy Spirit as well as dealing with the demonic in the healing-prayer process.) We must be aware of and cultivate their operation and allow them to flow as God intended. Scripture is clear on the operation and use of the gifts of the Holy Spirit in 1 Corinthians 12–14. People of evangelical persuasion typically have not been taught and properly schooled in their use and operation. Those of a more charismatic persuasion have operated more in the gifts but may have a hard time allowing the subtler, non-directive operation of the gifts in a Mind Renewing Healing Prayer session. For instance, they may want to give a word of knowledge, which may cause them to be inappropriately directive in the Mind Renewing Healing Prayer process. An example might be suggesting to a prayer ministry recipient, "I sense that you may have been sexually abused as a child by your grandfather," when the recipient has not brought that memory information into the prayer ministry session. This information, or word of knowledge, may or may not be true. The point is I do not want to direct the process and especially do not want to *suggest* memory content they have not presented. In the Mind Renewing Healing Prayer process, memory content should only emerge from the prayer recipient, not the minister. If I suggest memory content, I violate the will of the prayer recipient. God does not do this. I believe the prayer recipient will remember what they need to remember when they are ready to do so. The Mind Renewing Healing Prayer process helps facilitate their healing as the memories that need to come up emerge. Also, you cannot be accused of suggesting memory content if you haven't suggested what you think may have happened to the prayer recipient. We should follow and help them process only what they share with us.

In the same way, we must also let the prayer recipient grapple with their memory's validity. It is not the prayer minister's job or responsibility to determine the validity of, for instance, a sexual abuse memory. In reality, only the prayer recipient and God know the truth. The prayer minister does not know what transpired in the memory because they were not there.

In conclusion, when we learn to recognize and deal with these common hindrances, we will experience far greater success in receiving as well as ministering Mind Renewing Healing Prayer. I find that people move much more quickly through their memory content, identify their lies, and find peace when they are aware of these potential blocks and hindrances.

CHAPTER 12

HEALING TESTIMONIES

"The Lord says, 'I will give you back what you lost
to the swarming locusts, the hopping locusts,
the stripping locusts, and the cutting locusts.
It was I who sent this great destroying army against you.
Once again you will have all the food you want,
and you will praise the Lord your God,
who does these miracles for you.
Never again will my people be disgraced.
Then you will know that I am among my people Israel,
that I am the Lord your God, and there is no other.
Never again will my people be disgraced.'
(JOEL 2:25-27, NLT)

HEALING PRINCIPLE: God brings healing in extraordinary ways. I have been privileged to participate with the Lord in ministering healing through Mind Renewing Healing Prayer, to His people almost daily since 1999. There is a greater level of emotional healing available than many believe through our Lord and Savior Jesus Christ! He is not only risen, He is alive and present in a tangible way every day here on Earth. He is always present in my office as I minister healing to the emotionally wounded and broken. I am continuously amazed by the breakthrough people regularly experience through Mind Renewing Healing Prayer. I invite you to witness the wondrous work of the Lord's healing hand through the following testimonies.

Darlene's Story

When Darlene came to see me, she was depressed, distraught and in crisis. She was an attractive, elegant, soft-spoken woman of 51. Twice divorced, she was mystified by the poor choices she had made in marriage partners; she had seen two marriages crash and burn, one with an abusive, alcoholic husband who had betrayed her. We spent two eight-hour days together as I ministered Mind Renewing Healing Prayer to her. In that time, I learned that her parents divorced when she was two years old and that she was essentially abandoned by her dad. She had been molested at age twelve by a cousin, for which she still felt shame and self-contempt. Her mother also suffered from depression and emotional problems, and Darlene lived in fear that her mother would die. Her mother would often get mad at her, withdrawing from Darlene and refusing to speak to her for days at a time. In session, Darlene and I worked through memories of her mother's emotional abandonment and helped her identify her core beliefs. We discovered that Darlene had internalized the lie that she was worthless; it was awesome to behold the moment when Jesus communicated His love for her, declaring that she was worthy to him.

We worked through other memories where peers had rejected and treated her badly in school. She internalized other beliefs that "she didn't have any friends," "she was ugly and invisible," and "didn't have anything to offer." It was amazing to see the Lord invade these memories with a revelation of His truth. He revealed how He saw her and about how much she mattered to Him. He revealed to Darlene, as a little girl, the depth of His love for her.

While in session, Darlene remembered an encounter with her father when she was seven years old. While visiting her cousin's house on the Fourth of July, her father finally came to the family holiday picnic. She was so excited to see her dad, but sadly, he never acknowledged her. This reinforced and solidified the curse he had already communicated to her over the years. She was filled with deep feelings of rejection and disappointment. Seven-year-old Darlene vowed and concluded that "if she were prettier he would have noticed; if her short hair were longer he would notice her." As I asked Jesus to reveal His truth, she powerfully experienced the presence and love of Jesus in the memory. Instantly, her father's blatant rejection no longer mattered to seven-year-old Darlene. That truth was uploaded to her as an adult and something shifted within her. Her feelings of abandonment, rejection, shame, ugliness and worthlessness melted away in His glorious Presence. Jesus sat beside her in the memory and communicated His love for her and told her that He was there. (Jesus often communicates to us in memory during the Mind Renewing Healing Prayer process where He was that we didn't perceive at the time.) During our two-day healing-prayer session, in memory after memory, her pain melted away. The best thing about the healing process is that Jesus' truth uploads into our present-day life, producing permanent change and transformation. Only an encounter with God can do that. Below is a testimony that she sent to me almost two years later. When I communicated with her again in 2017, her family, marriage and personal life were prospering and she was still walking in freedom!

Dear Frank,

I was blessed to have counseling with you early last year, 2011. I have wanted to write this for a very long time and apologize for not sending it sooner. I had so much pain in my life. I loved Jesus so much yet found myself a divorced woman twice. How could this be? I asked myself. I had made very poor choices and had a great fear of abandonment. After having a two-day session with you I can truly say I went home a much stronger person and ready to face the world as a single woman of 51. Jesus showed me through Theophostic healing that He really was there beside me through all the pain I had experienced as a young child and adult. I felt healing in my heart take place and a light was able to shine through the darkness. It literally felt as though a grey sky of darkness was replaced with light as you gently allowed me to find the deep hurt and release it. I am happy to say nearly two years later that I am in a much better place in my life! I learned to be alone and an amazing thing happened...I'm very happy to say....After much prayer and healing, God brought a wonderful man into my life who is a true man of God and treats me like a princess. We are now married and equally yoked. I am a better mom to my children and enjoying life and my horses again. You helped me, through God's healing, to realize I should not have been abused. I want to add, however, that I now realize no one can complete us, not a spouse or a career—true completion comes from Jesus and a healed heart that recognizes this. Frank, I thank you for helping me to fully understand these things. God bless you.

Warmly,

– DARLENE FROM PA

Joan's Story

I once worked with a woman name Joan. When she came for healing sessions, she was deeply wounded and in distress. She was very emotionally stirred up after hearing some testimonies of people in her church who had been healed from childhood sexual abuse through Mind Renewing Healing Prayer. It was recommended that she come to do some healing sessions with me. She came in with fear and trepidation. Her inner mind knew the trauma that she had undergone in her childhood, even though she had partially dissociated it. As we began our sessions, after some initial resistance, she quickly engaged her deepest will in the Mind Renewing Healing Prayer process. Week after week, we went to her deeply buried and dissociated traumatic memories from her childhood. Every week she would come in for her session and I would give her a choice. "Would you like to do healing prayer today or talk?" Obviously I had already explained to her that the more healing prayer she did, the greater the breakthrough she was likely to experience. She chose, week after week, to go to the places of severe physical, emotional and sexual abuse trauma. For the first time in her life, in her early 60s, she began to experience tremendous breakthroughs.

Her family relationships and her sense of self-esteem, worth and value blossomed like flowers in the spring! She chose to go down the throat of the dog, so to speak. She chose to go to the depths of her being, to her painful, dissociated, sexual trauma memories that were buried deeply within. They were now leaking and stealing the quality of life God had intended for her. Her healing and transformation were glorious to behold. Weekly she journeyed with God in my office to the depths of her trauma, confronting her lie-based thinking, which resulted in dramatic breakthrough, healing and peace.

About a year ago I actually made an appointment and went in to see Frank. I wanted to find out if he could help me. I had watched him minister for about 5 years—even went to two of his seminars on Theophostic Prayer Ministry. I watched others that I knew who were seeing him. I watched with amazement at their growth and transformation. Maybe he could help me. It was worth a try.

At the time, I was miserable. I was depressed. I felt like I lived behind a wall of Plexiglas that I could never break through. I was there but not always totally engaged. I felt like I missed God's best for me—like I had failed him (and everyone else in my life). I had recently been having panic attacks and confusion. Yet, I could not put my finger on what would possibly be the cause.

I was 64 and happily married for many years. My husband and I raised three children who are all nicely married and have given us 8 beautiful grandchildren. I was enjoying being retired.

I had become a Christian at eight years of age. Always loved the Lord. Tried to do what was right. Received the Baptism of the Holy Spirit when I was in my twenties. With my husband, I owned a Christian bookstore and ministered full time. Received a degree in Biblical Studies and a certificate in Early

Childhood Development. Used both of those to the best of my ability. Was ordained and for a time an associate pastor.

So why was I so very miserable? And, why couldn't I climb out of that pit? Why did I feel like I had to strive just to get through each day?

I got tired of the battle and I gave up and went to see Frank.

That's when the Holy Spirit showed me the lies that I had believed because of my abusive upbringing. The lies lay buried in the core of my being. Even though my head knew God's truth and God's Word, they hadn't replaced the lies that I took in as a child.

Week by week the Holy Spirit revealed the lies and Frank guided me straight to Jesus and His truth. Week by week the walls came down, the lies exposed, and freedom came. Now I can believe and experience the love of my heavenly Father. I realized that I could be a human "being," not a human "doing."

More balance came into my life. I can say no, and I can say yes. It is even okay to have fun. I am more present in all situations. One of the grandest experiences has been my ability to feel—to feel more emotion, to feel life, to notice details of color and smell. I even dilly-dally and not feel guilty! And I am trying all sorts of new things. Something I would never have done before.

I am so thankful for Frank's ministry, his easy manner, and expertise. But thankful most of all for his willingness to listen and wait on the Holy Spirit with this patient.

— JOAN FROM VIRGINIA

Sean's Story

Sean and his wife were a young missionary couple. She was in her late twenties and Sean was in his early thirties. In the midst of the stress of being in a primitive African culture for four years, many of their unresolved wounds and hurts came bubbling to the surface. We worked on his issues of depression and low self-esteem, rooted in abandonment by his father. When he was young, his parents divorced, and he had little contact with his father. His mother was steeped in the hippie counterculture of the '60s and '70s, regularly smoked pot, and was involved in New Age. Sean's mother matured into a wonderful, godly woman after accepting Christ in later years. However, during his earlier years, the instability and abandonment from his parents deeply affected Sean, filling him with fear, low self-esteem and insecurity. This manifested through his difficulties with intimacy, depression and anger. This translated into increased marital conflict as his unresolved issues clashed with his wife's broken triggered areas.

Sean was willing to take the emotionally triggered reactions he was experiencing from his ministry and life stresses and pursue healing. The stress of living in a primitive, foreign land made life very difficult and challenging for him and his wife. As we processed through Sean's many memories, we discovered themes of abandonment, rejection and unworthiness. As Sean recognized the lies he had believed for most of his life, Jesus revealed His truth. From Sean's encounter with God, tremendous breakthrough occurred in his life. Today, Sean and his wonderful wife have two beautiful children. He has completed his PhD in theology, and he is pursuing a career teaching theology. He and his wife are building a great family and continuing on their sojourn into their God-given destiny! Sean later wrote to me:

My wife and I were serving as full-time missionaries and were recently married. It didn't take long before we both realized we had some things to work out in ourselves individually, as well as in our marriage. We fought quite frequently, and it was getting quite exhausting. While I went through Theophostic prayer with you, I came to see that the hurts and wounds of my childhood were affecting my relationships, especially with my wife. The fear of abandonment and neglect I experienced as a child caused me to put up walls and not open up to loved ones. The Lord came and spoke truth to my head and my heart, which has made all the difference in my relationships. Since Theophostic prayer, my relationship with my wife has deepened and gotten a lot better. I am trusting easier and learning to love her better. I would recommend any newly married couple or engaged couple to go through several sessions with you to have the Lord heal up any potential areas that would cause them to stumble or prevent the pure love of God to shine through.

– SEAN

Rachael's Story

I first met Rachael at a healing conference that I did in New England a number of years ago. I was invited to her church to do some Mind Renewing Healing Prayer training. I do healing-prayer demonstrations at my conferences, and I asked for volunteers. She volunteered, and I felt led by the Holy Spirit to choose her to do a healing-prayer demonstration. She had triggered emotions of anxiety, fear, shame and powerlessness that were manifesting in her current relationships. God did some significant healing during our healing session, but some troubling memories of abuse and trauma emerged that day at an early age that she had not previously fully remembered. A few months later, she called me and she flew to Virginia to do some intensive healing work at the Meadows Healing Prayer Center in Chesapeake, Virginia. For two full days, she worked through some deep, painful sexual abuse trauma and began to experience significant breakthrough. New confidence, peace and resolution in her life emerged and her extreme fear and anxiety subsided. She came back on a few different occasions over the years where God continued to do significant healing as she uncovered the root places in memory where her core lie-based beliefs were rooted. As Rachael pressed into her healing journey, she experienced tremendous breakthrough and her life was transformed. She has been very influential in leading others in her family and circle of friends to seek their own healing. Today she is a career and executive life coach, speaker and a powerful advocate for women in need of healing and restoration.

> *I was first introduced to Mind Renewing Healing Prayer in 2002 when Frank Meadows came to our church to teach on healing prayer. Shortly thereafter, I flew down to Virginia to receive Mind Renewing Healing Prayer ministry. Prior to the training, I had suffered with anxiety and fear since I was a small child. After receiving prayer ministry from Frank I felt like a backpack full of heavy weights had been lifted from me. I never realized how heavy the load was until it was lifted. I felt free, and with each passing day I realized that my life had changed. I no longer struggled with paralyzing fear and anxiety, and my relationship with my husband was better than I ever imagined. It has been 13 years, and I still am free; the triggers that so often plagued me are no longer part of my life. I thank God for this ministry and for Frank, who faithfully allows himself to be used of the Holy Spirit to bring lasting healing and change.*

> – RACHAEL FROM NEW ENGLAND

Sharon's Story

Before Sharon became my client, I saw her on a few occasions while covering for her therapist, my co-worker, who was on vacation. While working with her only a few times, I knew her to be a trauma client with Dissociative Identity Disorder (DID). I had become very discouraged with the progress I was seeing as a therapist working with trauma patients with DID, prior to learning the

Mind Renewing Healing Prayer principles. I was doing all I knew to do to integrate prayer, scripture, and the Holy Spirit's leading with sound therapeutic techniques, but with little breakthrough. I knew there was more, but I wasn't seeing it. I was very discouraged and burned out. For three years I stopped seeing trauma clients. Somewhere at the end of that period, a friend of mine brought Dr. Smith's Theophostic teachings to my attention. I started to study them and was excited to discover that I had finally found what I had been looking for. Jesus, through the Holy Spirit, was tangibly showing up during my times of ministry, and I was growing in co-laboring with Him in bringing healing to the brokenhearted! I was greatly encouraged, but I was neither ready nor willing to work with traumatized DID clients. Still, God has a way of divinely setting us up.

Sharon had left Virginia Beach for a few years, but when she moved back to the area she came to see me as a client. She seemed to be in a better place and told me that her DID had been "healed and resolved." I had my doubts about that, but it was true that she was not manifesting alter personalities as she had been before. As I shared with her about the healing-prayer approach I was now using, she expressed interest in trying the technique. In a short time, we began to see healing of her wounded memories. Then one day during a healing prayer session, her "healed" DID alter system emerged with a great deal of inner resistance. Unbeknownst to her outer mind, her deeply traumatized inner mind was now ready to do the deeper work of healing that needed to be done. The only problem was that I was not ready to do this deeper work as a therapist. I was in a quandary: I wanted to work with Sharon but I still wasn't open to working with DID. Ultimately, I wanted to help Sharon, so I decided to integrate all I knew about trauma and dissociation with my newly discovered healing-prayer approach. Over a two-year period, we visited many of Sharon's deeply hidden, dissociated sexual trauma memories. I learned and grew in helping her connect with the parts of herself she had buried for decades. Sharon came to see me weekly and experienced breakthrough as she chose to process through the pain of her broken places and as

Jesus revealed His truth to her in the process.

Up to this point, Sharon's life had included years of psychotherapy, a series of suicide attempts, many psychiatric hospitalizations, self-destructive behaviors, and unhealthy, broken relationships. Week after week, we processed through her horrific memories. We asked Jesus to reveal His marvelous truth to her core beliefs that anchored her in a deep sense of powerlessness, shame, self-hatred, fear and hopelessness. The Lord always revealed His truth to Sharon. As she released her anger and self-hatred, and forgave her abusers and herself,[1] she began to integrate her dissociated alter personalities back into her core personality. She found healing and wholeness, and a solid, integrated sense of self began to emerge. Near the end of our final sessions, Sharon moved about three hours away. She would often report her parts integrating into her core self as she drove home after sessions. God was doing a great work in her life, and it was glorious to behold. As of this writing, our work has been finished for at least 15 years. Today, Sharon lives a successful, productive, integrated life, working at a Christian University. She shares her perspective below:

> *I am a strong believer, advocate and testament of Theophostic counseling and the Lord's healing restoration. I spent approximately 30 years of my life in and out of psychiatric offices and institutions. I can't recall any 24-month period straight free of a hospitalization between the ages of 10 and 35. Dr. Smith refers to the revolving door of the same patients that never seemed to find true and lasting relief for years. That patient was me, over and over and over again, in and out of the struggle with deep depression, manic behavior, attempted suicides, with distorted irrational thinking and behavior. Some days I felt crazy and some days I knew I wasn't, as I tried to find a way to be a functioning youth, adult, wife, mother, employee, and Christian.*

---

[1] Obviously, abuse victims are not guilty for being abused. But because they may believe what happened to them was, on some level, their fault, I have them release their self-hatred to Jesus and walk through self-forgiveness if they so desire.

What was not accomplished in 30 years in and out of conventional counseling offices was healed and restored fully in just a few short years with Theophostic counseling. Like many who seek counseling, we know what happened (in generalities), we can identify the trauma (sometimes specifically), we can tell you what it was, how it felt and even express most of the details on one level or another. What we usually cannot understand is how it created the strange ways in which we perceive things around us and adapt to life based on those internal perceptions. For me, dissociation had so segregated the majority of my life that a memory of an entire 24-48 hour period without loss of several hours seldom occurred; it became my norm, and I really thought everyone's life was the same. In the course of working with Frank Meadows, we discovered coping mechanisms (personalities that identified themselves by their character traits, and some not so pleasant) that literally kept me alive, but also unintentionally or intentionally invited evil spirits of self-destruction, doubt and contempt.

Theophostic counseling restored my mind that was damaged between the ages of 3 to 7 by sexual abuse and I started my life at about 39 years old. Odd, but not uncomfortable to admit. As crazy as it sounds, I consider it a privilege to have walked through the torrential waters of my life and to have had the privilege to experience sitting with our Lord beside the still and peaceful waters that...brought to me...soundness of mind, an understanding of safety, and above all love—love greater than human capacity can fathom.

Today, I am employed at one of the largest and fastest growing Christian universities in the world. I stand in wonder that I am so privileged, and I marvel at the Lord's hand upon me, having kept me alive and on the special path He has me on.

– SHARON

These people are just a few of the thousands I have prayed with and ministered with Mind Renewing Healing Prayer since 1999. I see miracles and breakthrough regularly, often several times daily. It has been my privilege to co-labor with the Lord as He always makes His healing Presence available to whoever will choose to receive. I never tire of seeing the looks of deep distress, fear, sorrow, shame, hopelessness and anger quickly disappear as Jesus communicates His life-giving truth to the brokenhearted. In its place, I witness peace, calm, joy and resolution appear on the countenance of those who receive His truth in the dark inner recesses of the mind, as deep calls to deep, in past memories. As you see from these and many other testimonies throughout this book, the healing in these core foundational memories uploads to the present and translates to renewal of the mind and a transformed life. Praise the Lord for His faithfulness!

"The Lord is my Shepherd [to feed, guide, and shield me], I shall not lack. He makes me lie down in [fresh, tender] green pastures; He leads me beside the still and restful waters. He refreshes and restores my life (my self); He leads me in the paths of righteousness [uprightness and right standing with Him—not for my earning it, but] for His name's sake. Yes, though I walk through the [deep, sunless] valley of the shadow of death, I will fear or dread no evil, for You are with me; Your rod [to protect] and Your staff [to guide], they comfort me. You prepare a table before me in the presence of my enemies. You anoint my head with oil; my [brimming] cup runs over. Surely or only goodness, mercy, and unfailing love shall follow me all the days of my life, and through the length of my days the house of the Lord [and His presence] shall be my dwelling place."

(PSALM 23:1-6, AMPC)

EPILOGUE

BY FRANK MEADOWS

———————————————

"Pursue love, and desire spiritual gifts, but especially that you may prophesy…But he who prophesies speaks edification and exhortation and comfort to men. He who speaks in a tongue edifies himself, but he who prophesies edifies the church."

1 CORINTHIANS 14:1,3-4, NKJV

———————————————

Dear Reader,

I hope you have enjoyed *Jesus, Healer of the Brokenhearted.* I consider it to be an introduction to Mind Renewing Healing Prayer as well as a foundational piece in my series of writings on emotional healing and well-being. I have chosen to conclude this book with a letter to my readers that includes a final word regarding the healing journey. After the deep work of Mind Renewing Healing Prayer takes place, when lies have been exposed and God has revealed His truth to the prayer recipient, there is still more work to be done. This is because God intends for more than just our emotional healing. This is where the role of prophecy comes into play. God does not only want to heal and comfort; He wants to exhort and edify to launch us into our destiny! His desire is that we would live life abundantly in order to fulfill our God-given purposes. For this reason, I often use the end of a person's session to pray prophetically as the Holy Spirit leads.

During a Mind Renewing Healing Prayer session, I do not prophecy or directly give words of knowledge, because I am focused on helping the individual encounter the Presence of God and hear the Lord's voice. However, a closing prayer is a beautiful way to seal the time of ministry and to bless the work the Lord has done in the recipient's life. At that time, I allow myself to flow prophetically with the Spirit. As I pray, the Lord often brings scripture or images[1] that I may choose to share with the person. This prayer time may be anywhere from two to fifteen minutes, depending on the length of the session.

In my experience with Mind Renewing Healing Prayer, the Lord has taught me a few principles that I believe are important for ministers of healing prayer to consider. First, it is important to recognize that prophetic prayer is fundamentally different from Mind Renewing Healing Prayer, and so the two should not be intertwined. The purpose of healing is to renew minds and free people to walk in truth. The purpose of prophecy is to speak life, activate people and release them into their Kingdom destiny. Ultimately,

---

[1] Never suggestive memory content and I do not pray prophetically until the Mind Renewing Healing Prayer session is over.

prophetic words shift the atmosphere by releasing heavenly purposes, thereby bringing breakthrough into people's lives. I find that people who receive prophetic words from me tend to return later to tell me how encouraging the word has been in their lives and to their healing journey. I do not attribute this to myself, but rather the power of the Lord to speak clearly and directly through and to His people. I encourage recipients to record the word and listen to it at times when encouragement is needed in their life. Finally, because prophetic prayer is different in nature to healing prayer, it should never be used in a way that suggests memory content to the recipient. This is very important and, based on my clients' feedback, extremely helpful.

I can personally attest to the role that prophetic prayer has played in my life. In 1995, I made a trip to John and Carol Arnott's church, the Toronto Airport Christian Fellowship, to see and experience the Toronto Blessing revival. I had heard that the church was experiencing a mighty move of God that was impacting the world, so I chose to visit. While I was in a prayer meeting at the church, a French Canadian woman from Quebec, whom I had never met, began to prophecy over me. With her arms flailing and in a loud voice, she began to say that the Lord would use me for His glory and anoint me to write books. I thought the word sounded very cool, but at the time I didn't have anything significant to write. In fact, I didn't really like to write, other than what had been required of me at school.

I tucked this word away, pondered it and prayed about it from time to time over the years. Throughout the years, I heard similar words from other people who prayed for me. In August 2014, Isabel Allum prophesied over me for twelves minutes and the same themes emerged.

I hear the Lord saying to you, son, there are many things in you that need to be written. You have seen many things; you have heard many things. I saw you writing experiences, writing the journey, writing the books that need to be written. And as you write more is going to come and flow out of you. You have a lot to teach and a lot to give. There are many things you have tweaked that others need to learn. You have a great toolbox in you and that toolbox needs to be exposed to others. I saw you in training and equipping people in what you carry and, in doing that, God is going to add more on to you.

— ISABEL ALLUM, AUGUST 2014

Something was released and activated in me when Isabel released that word over my life. Within a month after her prophecy, I began to diligently write this book and have not stopped since. Now, I typically write five days a week. In the first year of writing, I supernaturally penned over 400 pages of writing. The content of those pages birthed this foundational piece on Mind Renewing Healing Prayer, as well as topics for other books still to come. I believe that God has given me that toolbox about which Isabel prophesied in 2014. My desire is to share it with you, and the rest of the Body of Christ, for the equipping of the saints. Like a carpenter who regularly adds new equipment to his toolbox so that he can accomplish more work, I will continue to write what the Lord has taught me so that others may be exposed to and use the unique tools with which He has equipped me.

My point in sharing my own story is that you will see that there is power in true prophetic words. They help shift the atmosphere in a way that brings life and activates the gifts, anointing and heavenly abilities that God has already placed within you. As you step into your own healing journey, I bless you to encounter powerful prophetic words that launch you into your God-given destiny. I bless you to receive, test and hold on to every word that is from God, treating them as seeds sown into the soil of your heart. I bless you to know God as both the awesome Author and the great Gardener, and to allow Him to write the story of your life and tend to the soil of your heart for your whole life long. As you seek your healing, may you come to know Him more intimately each day than the day before.

FRANK MEADOWS

ABOUT THE AUTHOR

Frank Meadows, LCSW, is the founder of the Meadows Healing Prayer Center in Chesapeake, Virginia. He has been a mental health professional since 1980, is a licensed clinical social worker, and for many years was the clinical director at Christian Psychotherapy Services. Since 1999 many people, including many in leadership, have come from across the United States and internationally to receive Frank's intensive inner-healing prayer ministry. He has ministered over 20,000 hours using Mind Renewing Healing Prayer with many experiencing dramatic life-changing results. He has extensive training in Theophostic Healing Prayer. His calling to the Body of Christ, and especially leadership, is to help others find wholeness in order to walk fully in their destiny. He has ministered and taught on emotional healing and Mind Renewing Healing Prayer training seminars throughout the United States, as well as in Turkey, Ghana, South Africa and Mozambique. Frank has taught at the Toronto Airport Christian Fellowship Kingdom Living School in Virginia Beach, Virginia; at Heidi Bakers' Iris Ministries Harvest Missions School in Mozambique, Africa; at the Leadership MetaFormation Institute in Redding, California, with Tony Stoltzfus; and at the Theophostic Prayer Ministry International Conventions. He has done several TV shows on healing with Isik Abla on her show *Embracing New Life*, broadcast throughout the United States, Africa and the Middle East. Frank is an elder and teacher at Big House Church in Norfolk, Virginia. He has been married to his wife, Beth, since 1976, who works at the Christian Broadcasting Network for Orphans Promise. They reside in Chesapeake, Virginia. They have two married adult sons, Ryan and his wife Catherine and Jonathan and his wife Anna.

ABOUT THE MEADOWS HEALING PRAYER CENTER

Meadows Healing Prayer Center is a healing prayer ministry with professional expertise based upon the principles of Mind Renewing Healing Prayer, a biblically-based, Holy Spirt-led approach to inner healing and mind renewal. Its founder, Frank Meadows, has ministered to thousands of people since 1999 with great results. Many people have reported breakthrough from a variety of emotional problems, brokenness, emotional pain, conflicted relationships and past abuse. The root of our brokenness is our lie-based core foundational beliefs or mental strongholds. They are formed in childhood as we make interpretations when we are wounded, hurt, rejected and abused. These lies are reinforced throughout our lives whenever our lies are triggered and activated. Many live in an unhealthy pattern of reenactment of their triggered reactions, therefore living a life of defeat. At the Meadows Healing Prayer Center, we help you take defeated, triggered life patterns and find mind renewal, healing and breakthrough to experience "beauty for ashes." As you face your triggered emotions, we help you choose to encounter our Lord and Savior Jesus Christ in the dark places of your past broken memories. As His truth and light melt away the lies of the past, the triggers resolve and defeated patterns change. The Meadows Healing Prayer Center is a safe, comfortable place to encounter His healing presence.

To learn more about the Meadows Healing Prayer Center, receive healing prayer ministry, and upcoming books and teachings by Frank Meadows, please visit http://www.meadowshealingprayercenter.com and sign up to be on the mailing list.